Invest For Change, Reap Financial Rewards,
and Increase Your Happiness

DO GOOD *while* DOING WELL

MARCIA DAWOOD

OFFICIAL WORKBOOK

Copyright © 2024 Marcia Dawood
marcia@marciadawood.com
www.marciadawood.com

All rights reserved. No part of this publication in print or in electronic format may be reproduced, stored in a retrieval system, or transmitted in any form or by any means, electronic, mechanical, photocopying, recording, or otherwise without the prior written permission of the publisher.

The scanning, uploading, and distribution of this book without permission is a theft of the author's intellectual property. Thank you for your support of the author's rights.

Editing, design, distribution by Bublish
Published by Do Good Media

ISBN: 978-1-64704-892-1 (paperback)

TABLE OF CONTENTS

Introduction | *v*

Part I: Find Your Why | *1*

Assess Your Current Involvement with Creating Change | *2*
Your Relationship with Money | *9*
Myths around Money and Angel Investing | *13*
Your Perception of Risk and Reward | *15*
Create Your Halo Strategy™ | *19*
The Value You Bring Beyond Dollars | *22*
Changes You Want to See | *25*
Find Your Why | *28*

Part II: Understand How to Find and Evaluate Deals | *29*

Where to Find Start-ups | *30*
The Initial Screening Process | *31*
Evaluate with Your Halo Navigator™ | *33*
Pitch Deck Critique | *35*
Your Opportunity to Review a Start-up | *48*
After the Pitch | *81*

Part III: Get Started | *85*

Invest with Your Time | *86*
Find an Angel Group | *90*
Diversify with Funds | *91*

Get Started with a Small Amount of Money and a Little Bit of Time | *91*

Debt Crowdfunding — Bonus Content not in the book, Do Good While Doing Well | *92*

Create a Mock Portfolio | *95*

Invest with Philanthropic Dollars | *100*

Invest from Your IRA | *102*

Tax Advantages for Angels | *104*

Time for Action | *105*

Making Investment Decisions with a Partner/Spouse or Family | *109*

Final Steps | *113*

A Favor | *117*

Let's Start a Conversation | *119*

Glossary | *121*

Author's Note | *127*

Acknowledgments | *129*

Author Bio | *131*

INTRODUCTION

I never thought, as one person, I could affect the change I want to see in the world. I thought that was for big companies and charities to work on. Not me. My career started in corporate America, working for the same company for more than sixteen years. And then, one day, I accepted an invitation to a meeting to hear a few entrepreneurs talk about their companies and the change they wanted to make in the world. I was fascinated. People were out there working on innovation near me? And they were interested in *my* help? How could I help entrepreneurs grow their businesses? What did I even know about entrepreneurship? And I didn't have the kind of money the people you see on shows like *Shark Tank* do, so how could it be for me? These and many other questions went through my head when I first learned about angel investing in 2012.

Through angel investing, I found and engaged with companies working on interesting innovations I cared about, which could make a real difference in the world. I met many types of people I never would have otherwise. And I discovered a way to use my time and dollars for change.

Additionally, we need to reframe our thinking around investing. Many people hear the word *investing* and think they must focus only on evaluating the potential financial gain. There's a common worry about feeling judged by others or doubting ourselves if investment choices don't yield anticipated financial outcomes. This mindset needs a refresh. Years ago, a returns-only focus might have had merit, but now there is more to it—our investments can have an impact beyond financial returns—we can make choices to *do good while doing well*.

We also need to shift our thinking about the burden we put on charities, believing they can solve the world's problems. In 2020, Americans donated $471 billion to charities. A record year, thanks to COVID, and that's *a lot* of money. Maybe you contributed as one of the donors. If so, do you know what your money was used for? Did you feel like you made a difference? I was shocked when I learned $471 billion represents *only about 1 percent* of the value of all the companies publicly traded on the US stock market. If we want to effect significant change, we need to look not just at nonprofits and place the burden on them but also at innovative for-profit companies creating positive change. Invest when they are small and help them grow.

Donating to charity isn't the only way to do good; traditional investing isn't the only way to do well. We can drive positive, impactful change, feel good about the entrepreneurs we are backing, and still seek financial returns.

Innovative start-ups are tackling major issues, like treatments for diseases and reducing poverty. Yet all too frequently, their groundbreaking ideas abandoned, metaphorically left on the cutting room floor, due to insufficient funding to turn these ambitious concepts into reality. Imagine the happiness and pride you would feel if you were part of advancing such transformative ventures, directly contributing to bringing life-changing ideas to fruition.

In 2023, there were only about 300,000 angel investors in the US, according to the Angel Capital Association (ACA). That is less than a fraction of one percent of the US population. We need more people to participate in supporting start-ups so that we can see change happen faster. And not just innovative changes in areas like health care and climate change. We also need to see changes in how much funding goes to underrepresented entrepreneurs, including women and people of color. According to Bloomberg, women receive less than 3 percent of venture capital funding, and people of color get much less than that. These disparities have persisted for many years. Imagine the innovations we are missing out on due to the lack of support for these ventures.

To change the amount of funding going to innovative companies, especially ones led by underrepresented founders, we must increase the number and diversity of people making these early-stage investment decisions. To do that, we need more people to become aware of their opportunities to participate in creating change through investment at all levels.

Many people I have spoken to over the years believe working with start-ups, especially investing in them, is meant only for the rich and well-connected. This is simply not true.

You may be wondering how. How can individuals make a real difference? For starters, in 2016, the Securities and Exchange Commission, where I sit on an advisory committee, changed the rules, so now just about anyone can invest in a start-up for as little as $50 through equity and debt crowdfunding. Plus, many other ways exist, which we will cover in this workbook.

My mission to raise awareness among people of all socioeconomic levels about their potential to become angel investors began on my podcast, *The Angel Next Door*, in 2021 and continues in my book, *Do Good While Doing Well: Invest for Change, Reap Financial Rewards, and Increase Your Happiness*, and now in this companion workbook.

In the first section of this three-part workbook, you will evaluate your current involvement in creating change, whether extensive or minimal. This may be something you've contemplated before or something that rarely crosses your mind, and either is perfectly fine. The activities in this section are designed to help you identify what matters most to you and where you might want to focus your time or money to drive change in those areas, even if you are unsure how at the start, which we will cover in Part III.

If you feel your past efforts haven't been sufficient, please set those feelings aside. You'll have the opportunity to develop a plan that reflects your values and how you can contribute meaningfully—including some new ideas you might not have considered before. These activities will help you assess what you find important, explore your attitudes toward money and risk, and identify patterns from your past behavior.

The second section of this workbook explores the criteria for selecting companies that align with your values and objectives. This section equips you with practical strategies and tools to evaluate potential investments by analyzing an overview of two different companies.

In the third section, you will finalize your plans to take action. Whether you begin by exploring start-up activity in your local area, mentoring an entrepreneur, or joining a local angel group, you'll be equipped with numerous options. From equity crowdfunding platforms where you will create a mock portfolio to exploring how to use philanthropic dollars and retirement accounts to invest, you'll uncover various avenues to make a meaningful impact while pursuing potential financial returns.

Some activities in this workbook might be enjoyable and productive when done with a partner, friend, or family member. Feel free to involve them in your process. If you need guidance on initiating those conversations, refer to the section at the end of Part III titled "Making Investment Decisions with a Partner/Spouse or Family."

Although I strive to avoid using acronyms or terms without explanations, you'll find a glossary at the end of the workbook to help clarify any terms you may be unfamiliar with.

Of course, readers should consult their own tax, investing, legal, or accounting advisors before making important financial decisions.

Your journey to make a difference, get financial rewards, and increase your happiness begins within the pages of the book *Do Good While Doing Well* and this official accompanying workbook.

Part I

FIND YOUR WHY

In this section, you will:

- Assess Your Current Involvement with Creating Change
    - Your Relationship with Money
    - Myths Around Money and Angel Investing
    - Your Perception of Risk and Reward

- Create your Halo Strategy™
    - The Value You Bring Beyond Dollars
    - Changes You Want to See

- Find Your Why

This workbook will take you on a journey with opportunities to answer questions, reflect on past experiences, and journal through writing and/or drawing. Feel free to customize your experience with the activities and exercises. While they're structured logically, feel empowered to make them your own. You can follow through with all the activities and prompts or skip those that don't resonate. Feel comfortable exploring what feels most relevant and meaningful to you.

Before diving into your investing journey, taking the time for self-reflection can be incredibly beneficial. Understanding your motivations, values, and past experiences will provide a strong foundation and clearer direction for your future investments. A reflection box at the end of each section will help you tie all your thoughts together and ensure that your investment decisions align with your personal goals and values.

ASSESS YOUR CURRENT INVOLVEMENT WITH CREATING CHANGE

To discover your WHY or motivation for driving change, let's start by assessing your current involvement with the changes you want to see—those you are most passionate about. This will help you understand your motivations. We will also examine your current feelings toward money and risk.

Looking back, I wish I had developed a clear strategy sooner for allocating my resources—both time and money—to the changes close to my heart. My journey began with charitable donations and eventually evolved to include investing in early-stage companies that were solving problems I cared about.

Finding your WHY will lay the foundation for designing a roadmap to investing for change. We will call this your Halo Strategy™.

For reference, here are eight common Halo Themes™ or areas of change (in no particular order) that might help stimulate your thinking…

8 Common Halo Themes

01.  **Promote Equity/Equality**

02. **Minimize Food Insecurity**

03.  **Reduce Poverty/ Decrease the Wealth Gap**

04.  **Enhance Environmental Sustainability**

05.  **Support Health and Well-Being**

06.  **Improve Educational Quality**

07.  **Promote Thriving Communities**

08.  **Encourage Innovation**

 www.marciadawood.com

Let's start to design your Halo Strategy™ by assessing your current involvement.

Activity: List any positive changes you're currently supporting or have supported in the past, including volunteering, investing, donating, and advocating—this could be in your job/career and your community. Maybe the Halo Themes™ sparked your thinking to include new areas you would like to support. After you have brainstormed your list, put a star next to the top three you are most passionate about.

Feel free to express your answers in the space provided. You can write and/or draw, so the lines are not as dark.

Activity: Go back to your list and jot down an estimate of how much time you dedicate(d) monthly/annually to supporting these changes. Don't worry if you find some causes you care about but you haven't known how to take action yet.

People are driven by various motivations to get involved with changes or causes they care about. Let's call them the Halo Motivators™. Here are ten common reasons that inspire individuals to take action:

10 Halo Motivators™

1. Personal Connection
Personal experiences, like a family member's illness, often motivate people to support related causes.

2. Desire to Make a Difference
A desire to make the world a better place drives individuals to engage with various causes.

3. Social Influence
Seeing others involved can inspire more to join, driven by social influence and community.

4. Ethical or Moral Beliefs
Personal convictions about justice, equality, or environmental conservation can motivate action aligned with ethical beliefs.

5. Community Impact
Desire for community improvements motivates involvement in local, national, global, or affinity group causes.

6. Educational Interest
Pursuit of knowledge can lead people to engage with causes that deepen their understanding or apply their skills.

7. Professional Development
Opportunities for networking, skill development, or resume' enhancement can motivate participation in charitable activities.

8. Emotional Response
Emotional reactions, like compassion for disaster victims or anger at social injustices, can drive immediate involvement.

9. Legacy Building
The desire to leave a positive mark and improve the world for the next generation can motivate long-term commitment to a cause.

10. Religious or Spiritual Beliefs
Religious or spiritual beliefs can drive acts of charity and service.

Understanding these motivations can help individuals better align their actions with their values, leading to more sustained and fulfilling involvement in the changes they care about moving forward.

Below is a table that lets you rank your motivations for getting involved with a cause. The ranking is on a scale from 1 to 5, where 1 indicates the least influence and 5 indicates the most influence.

Halo Motivator™ Ranking Worksheet

ACTIVITY: FILL IN YOUR RANKINGS TO DETERMINE WHAT YOUR TOP THREE HALO MOTIVATORS ARE.

THE RANKING IS ON A SCALE FROM 1 TO 5, WHERE 1 INDICATES THE LEAST INFLUENCE AND 5 INDICATES THE MOST INFLUENCE.

MOTIVATION	RANKING (1-5)
Personal Connection	
Desire to Make a Difference	
Social Influence	
Ethical or Moral Beliefs	
Community Impact	
Educational Interest	
Professional Development	
Emotional Response	
Legacy Building	
Religious or Spiritual Beliefs	

List your top three motivations below and the top three changes you care about from the list you made in the previous activity. Do your top three changes align with your top three motivations?

Activity: Recall moments or experiences in your life that have influenced your perspective on the changes you want to see in the world. Write or draw your recollections below.

Activity: In the past, have you set specific goals or measured the impact of your contribution to these changes? How did you do that?

Activity: Were your expectations met? Were there challenges? How did you feel about what you contributed then? How do you feel now?

Reflection: Review and reflect on your responses from this section to assess your current involvement in areas where you want to see change. What are your takeaways? Would others agree that your takeaways are in line with your personality, beliefs, and view on the world?

YOUR RELATIONSHIP WITH MONEY

Before proceeding further, let's take a moment to reflect on our emotional relationship with money. This workbook focuses on how and why to invest in the change you want to see in the world.

If we all talked about money and investing more openly, discussing how much or how often someone invests and the reasons behind those choices wouldn't seem strange or uncomfortable. Money can be a difficult topic because everyone has a different relationship with it. People are often judged whether they have a lot or a little, and rarely is there a happy medium. Regardless of one's wealth, there will always be someone with more and someone with less. By talking about money more often, we can learn how to better communicate about investing, especially investing for change.

Money holds a unique place in our lives, influencing our financial decisions, emotions, beliefs, and sense of security. Our attitudes towards money are often shaped by our upbringing, experiences, and cultural influences, leading to a complex web of thoughts and feelings surrounding this resource. Understanding and acknowledging these feelings and that there is not a universal "right" answer, can help us make more informed and aligned investment decisions.

In the following activities, I invite you to examine your relationship with money more deeply, exploring your beliefs, values, and behaviors related to financial matters. Reflecting on your thoughts toward money and investing can help you align your money habits with your values and aspirations, regardless of whether you seek financial abundance, security, or freedom. However, money can bring up unpleasant feelings. So, if you become uncomfortable, I encourage you to take your time. By reflecting on your past experiences, current attitudes, and future aspirations, you can gain valuable insights into your money mindset and uncover any hidden barriers or opportunities for growth.

> *Activity*: Reflect on your earliest memories or experiences with money. This could be from your childhood or maybe the first time you earned money. How have these experiences shaped your current beliefs and attitudes toward money?

Activity: List a few of your values when it comes to money. Some examples would be security, freedom, generosity, legacy, and independence—just to name a few. Reflect on why or how much these values are important to you.

Activity: Identify one to three short-term and one to three long-term financial goals. Describe why each goal is important to you.

Activity: List three to five ways you currently spend or invest your money. Reflect on how these expenditures align with your values and priorities, and consider any adjustments you might want to make moving forward.

Activity: Reflect on when you achieved a dream goal involving money. Describe the goal, the steps you took to reach it, and how it felt to accomplish it. Consider what this experience taught you about setting financial goals and aligning your spending or investments with your dreams.

Reflection: Review and reflect on your responses from this section and what impact they have on your relationship with money. What are your takeaways?

MYTHS AROUND MONEY AND ANGEL INVESTING

While *Do Good While Doing Well* explores various aspects of investing beyond monetary gain, it's important to recognize the significance of financial rewards, as, ultimately, angels seek those, too.

One of the top questions I get about angel investing is, "Isn't this only for rich people?" For the most part, that used to be true because private investment was restricted to people with a certain level of wealth. However, three significant changes have occurred since 2016, making early-stage investing more accessible. Few people know about these changes.

1. The Securities and Exchange Commission (SEC) changed the rules, and now anyone can invest in a private company for as little as $50 through equity and debt-based crowdfunding.

2. Philanthropic dollars (money generally used to donate to charity) can be used to invest in a start-up and still get a tax write-off by using a donor-advised fund (DAF). Any financial gains would be put back into the DAF for future use and not returned to the donor (more on this in Part III).

3. Revenue-based financing (RBF) allows the investor to lend money to a start-up and be paid back each month by the company. The company shares a percentage of the revenue with the investor until the loan is paid off (more on this in Part III).

Why does the perception that investing in private companies is only for the rich persist? In addition to limited awareness of the 2016 rule changes, the SEC previously imposed wealth-based requirements on who could participate in private investments by establishing an *accredited investor* definition. While these restrictions were intended to ensure that people had sufficient financial means to bear the financial risks of early-stage investing, they also limited those who could gain the upside of these investments. The name alone "accredited investor" is confusing since the word accredited leads some to believe an accreditation or certification of some kind is required—which may also include classes or exam(s).

The accredited investor definition as of this writing is based mainly on income and wealth levels. The investor must make an annual income of $200,000 if single ($300,000 with a spouse) or have $1 million in net worth, excluding the primary home. A few years ago, the definition was expanded slightly to include a few measures of sophistication such as certain financial licenses. You can find the most recent definition on my website at www.marciadawood.com/dogood.

When the definition of an accredited investor is discussed, feelings come up around money. I remember when my husband, Izzy, and I were first invited to an angel group meeting, we had to acknowledge that we met the definition of an accredited investor. This felt strange—as if we had to prove our worthiness to attend this meeting based on our level of income or wealth. This is why I don't want the definition to be focused just on money. Just because someone has money doesn't magically make them a smart investor. Seems like a dumb rule. Shouldn't more education be involved?

And this isn't just about feelings toward money. The word *investing* can carry different meanings. It extends beyond monetary transactions, including investing time for personal growth or emotional well-being. Unfortunately, many individuals associate investing solely with financial gains, which can lead to apprehension and fear of failure. This narrow perception overlooks the intrinsic benefits and non-monetary returns investments can yield. The fear of being perceived as unintelligent or having made a poor decision due to a lack of financial returns often discourages people from exploring investment opportunities fully. This is true for potential angel investors too.

YOUR PERCEPTION OF RISK AND REWARD

Deeply ingrained beliefs about money intersect with our attitudes and perceptions towards risk and reward in using our money and investing. Your responses to the activities about money could shed light on how you view risk-taking in financial matters. Positive experiences, such as successful investments or financial gains, may bolster confidence and encourage you to take on greater risks with some of your investments. Conversely, negative experiences, such as losses or financial setbacks, can instill fear and caution, leading to a more risk-averse mindset—or we could call it risk-astute, which usually means we want to be cautious and have more information before making an investment decision.

Even individuals who consider themselves risk-averse make significant decisions that involve managing risks, such as buying a house, getting married, or having children. This demonstrates that risk levels don't preclude one from becoming an angel investor; they require thoughtful risk management aligned with personal goals. Understanding your comfort with risk will help shape your investment strategy without limiting your possibilities.

Investing comes with risk. The level of risk is different depending on the type of investment. The financial return on investment (ROI) is usually commensurate with the level of risk. Buying a U.S. government bond can have a low risk, and with that could come a lower possible return than, say, a public stock, which could have higher risk but could also have higher returns.

In Chapter One of *Do Good While Doing Well*, I referenced a conversation between my husband and me in which I asked him to explain alternative assets related to investing and risk. "They are things like art, collectibles, and real estate," he explained. "Alternative assets are increasingly appealing to investors seeking diversification beyond traditional options like stocks and mutual funds. This attractiveness stems from their lack of correlation with the conventional market. For instance, the value of a piece of art hinges on the dynamics of supply and demand within the art market, as well as the artist's popularity, rather than being influenced by corporate earnings or economic updates. Additionally, a diverse array of asset types ensures a more balanced portfolio. This diversification strategy reduces the risk of financial loss, as it avoids the pitfall of concentrating all investments in a single area or putting all your eggs in one basket."

Angel investments are a form of alternative assets. Many alternative assets lack liquidity, meaning you can't buy and sell your ownership stake quickly and easily for cash, as you can with public stocks on platforms like E-trade. The lack of liquidity is why many angels limit their investments in early-stage companies to just five to ten percent of their investable assets and set a maximum dollar amount for these investments.

It's crucial to recognize that our feelings about money and risk are not static; they evolve over time in response to life events, financial circumstances, and personal growth. By understanding the underlying beliefs and emotions driving our attitudes toward money and risk, we can cultivate a more informed and empowered approach to investing. This introspective journey lays the foundation for making strategic investment decisions aligned with our values, goals, and aspirations.

Activity: Think of a time when you made a decision or investment in something you cared deeply about that involved risk, whether financial or not. How did you manage that risk, and what were the outcomes?

Activity: Reflect on your feelings about risk and reward when investing. How comfortable are you with the risk/reward ratios related to investing? How has your risk tolerance changed in the last five years, if it has?

Activity: Reflect on a time when you avoided taking a risk. What motivated your decision? How did you feel afterward?

Activity: Explore past experiences or beliefs that may contribute to your risk/reward comfort levels. How do these experiences shape your approach to investing in both the short and long term?

Reflection: Review and reflect on your responses in this section about your feelings related to risk and reward. What are your takeaways?

CREATE YOUR HALO STRATEGY™

Now that you have reflected on past experiences in change-making, relationships with money, and risk/reward, let's look to the future to begin to create your Halo Strategy™.

I wished I had a strategy when investing in early-stage companies in 2012. I invested quite a bit of time and some money without thinking about the big picture and how this would fit into what I really cared about and what change I wanted to see. Initially, I was eager to learn, so I would take coffee meetings with just about any entrepreneur. I made time and financial investments without having all the facts. I had "shiny-object syndrome." Or in this case, shiny-*halo* syndrome. I would get involved even if it didn't fit into my *investment thesis*. Every money manager, whether of mutual funds or pension funds, has an investment thesis. Experienced investors will have a clear plan that details specifics about what they will and won't invest in: the type of company, how developed the business is, and how much money they are willing to commit—all these things would go into an *investment thesis*. I didn't know this when I got started. I would see a company or founder I liked and make my decision. This workbook will help you create your investment thesis, or what we will call your *halo strategy*.

Looking back, I was missing a guide I could use before investing time or money. A guide to help me decide what I cared about the most, how much I was willing to contribute in hours and dollars, and ways I could increase my exposure to more companies and decrease my risk of losses. I created a guide for you to use throughout this workbook—it's called the Halo Strategy™ worksheet.

This worksheet will help you create an outline of what you truly care about, the changes you would like to see in the world, and a plan for being that change. You will learn how you can use your time, money, expertise, or all the above to achieve financial gains, emotional rewards, or both! You will be ready to realize your invest-for-change potential.

On the next page is the Halo Strategy™ worksheet—your Be-the-Change plan. Feel free to fill this out right in the workbook. You'll revisit this worksheet as you progress through the workbook, using it as an overall summary of all your reflections, activities, or prompts. Think of it as a one-page wrap-up summarizing your journey.

NAME _____ DATE _____

HALO STRATEGY™ WORKSHEET

How I Want to Contribute

Changes I Want to See in the World

My Valuable Skills

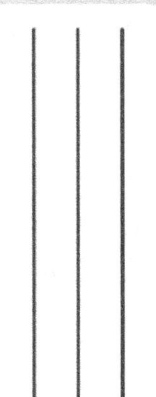

How Much Time/Money I will Start with

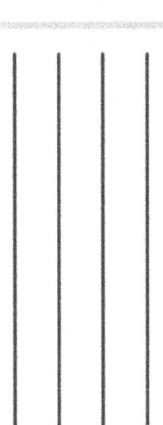

When I will Start

ACTION PLAN

1.
2.
3.

THIS IS YOUR BE-THE-CHANGE PLAN

www.marciadawood.com

© 2024 Marcia Dawood

THE VALUE YOU BRING BEYOND DOLLARS

I quickly learned that, yes, start-up companies need money, but they need a lot more than just money. Entrepreneurs are usually very good at their craft, but sometimes, they aren't so good at all of the business parts. So, being an angel can mean investing money, time, and expertise, or all the above. You don't need to have a PhD or be an intellectual property attorney to offer a company your expertise. You could be someone with bookkeeping experience or you may have worked in human resources. These skills are extremely valuable to a start-up. Building a company is hard work and often takes a village.

To begin filling out your worksheet, let's start by identifying your skills that could be valuable to a start-up. For me, I'm good with spreadsheets and numbers. I have helped a few companies with simple financial projections. I'm also a good listener, and although I'm not a therapist, I have helped company founders just by giving them a shoulder to lean on.

Activity: Reflect on your past experiences, achievements, interests, or hobbies. What unique skills or expertise have you developed? This could be in your work life or personal life.

Activity: Consider the challenges or problems you've successfully navigated in the past. How did you overcome them, and what skills did you leverage in the process?

Activity: Reflect on feedback you've received from colleagues, friends, or mentors on your skills and talents. Are there any recurring themes or strengths that stand out, indicating areas where you could add value to a start-up?

Reflection: Review and reflect on your responses from this section about the value you bring beyond dollars. What are your takeaways?

Now, summarize the most important skills or contributions you believe you have that would add value to a start-up. No skill is too big or too small. Once you are done, put your answers in the "My Valuable Skills" box of the Halo Strategy™ worksheet.

CHANGES YOU WANT TO SEE

In previous exercises, you assessed your current involvement, if any, in creating change. You may have identified the changes or causes that ignite your heart. As a reminder, on page 3, we introduced the eight Halo Themes™ or areas of change (in no particular order) that people often look at to see change—but you don't need your passions to fit into these categories.

Activity: Consider your personal experiences and values. What issues or causes resonate with you on a deeper level? Are there any specific challenges or injustices you've witnessed or experienced firsthand that you feel passionate about addressing? Look back at the list of Halo Motivators™ for reference.

Activity: Think about the communities or groups of people you care about. What are the most pressing issues facing these communities, and how could you play a role in addressing them?

Activity: Consider the long-term impact you hope to have on the world. What legacy do you want to leave behind, and what steps can you take now to work toward that vision?

Reflection: Review and reflect on your responses from this section about the changes you want to see. What are your takeaways?

Now, summarize the changes you want to see. Once you are done, put your answers in the "Changes I Want to See in the World" box of the Halo Strategy™ worksheet.

FIND YOUR WHY

After completing the exercises and reflections, you've likely gained valuable insights into your personal motivations and the changes you aspire to see in the world. By exploring your experiences, values, and skills, you've uncovered your "why"—the driving force behind your desire to make a difference. Armed with this understanding, you're better equipped to define your purpose and take meaningful action toward effecting positive change.

Part II of this workbook will explore the criteria for selecting companies that align with your values and objectives. This section will equip you with practical strategies and tools to evaluate potential investments and ensure they resonate with your vision for positive change. In Part III, you will have the opportunity to complete your Halo Strategy™ worksheet by uncovering the diverse opportunities that have emerged, especially since 2015, for investing in start-up companies with your time and/or money. From equity crowdfunding platforms to impact investment funds, you'll discover avenues to make a meaningful impact while pursuing financial returns and you will be on your way to taking action!

Part II

UNDERSTAND HOW TO FIND AND EVALUATE DEALS

Now that you have figured out your why, you may wonder: How do I meet interesting start-up companies, and how do I decide which companies or funds are worth investing my time, talent, or treasure in helping? In this section we will cover:

- Where to Find Start-ups
- The Initial Screening Process
- Evaluate with Your Halo Navigator™
- Pitch Deck Critique – Your Opportunity to Review a Start-up
- After the Pitch

WHERE TO FIND START-UPS

Start-ups exist in almost every city and every town. We will review in more detail in Part III of the workbook about where you can find them, but one way is through angel groups. These groups pool their resources and expertise to collaboratively evaluate start-up companies and make investment decisions together. Some are based on geographic region and some are based on industries of interest such as life sciences or healthcare. Finding an angel group can be done by searching on the internet or by going to the website of the Angel Capital Association (ACA) at angelcapitalassociation.org. Angels can pool their resources through a fund as well. Typically, a fund has a fund manager or investment committee who decides what to invest in, and the investors, or Limited Partners (LPs) as they are called, are more passive.

You may be wondering—how do angel groups or funds find start-ups? Entrepreneurs can usually apply directly through an angel group or fund's website; however, angels tend to refer companies to each other because typically one angel group cannot fund the entire amount of capital a company is looking for at any given time. The ACA, whose members consist of angel groups, funds, and individual angels, has established peer groups around certain types of investments, such as industry, regional location, or women-led companies. Finding start-ups can come in many forms.

Another example of how founders and funders can be matched is Scroobious. Allison Byers, a member of the ACA's DEI committee, created Scroobious, an AI-powered, algorithmic-driven platform designed to connect founders and investors with a strong mission to increase diversity in the start-up ecosystem. For founders, Scroobious offers an innovative space to create pitches that truly resonate with potential investors, significantly increasing their chances of securing funding. The platform provides comprehensive fundraising guidance where founders can refine and elevate their pitches through a combination of online learning and professional feedback on draft material, ensuring they stand out in the competitive start-up landscape.

For investors, Scroobious enhances the investment pipeline by offering AI-powered personalized curation. This feature matches investors with start-ups based on both business metrics and the founders' characteristics, ensuring that diverse, high-potential opportunities are not overlooked. The scalable online marketplace connects start-ups and angels at the right moment, facilitating meaningful discussions that can lead to successful funding outcomes. By bridging the gap between diverse founders and investors, Scroobious is driving significant change and promoting inclusivity within the start-up ecosystem.

THE INITIAL SCREENING PROCESS

Most early-stage companies are just that—early, and a spectrum of development stages exists, ranging from emerging start-ups to more established entities. This means that each company has varying degrees of professional maturity, shown by factors, such as team composition, product development, and customer acquisition. In this section, I'll provide you with guidelines, probing questions, and illustrative examples to aid in the process of starting to evaluate companies or "deals" as we call them. There are two stages of evaluation—screening and due diligence.

Angel groups and funds may examine hundreds of companies annually before deciding to invest in a handful. If you think of a funnel, the widest part is the number of start-ups that apply for funding. As they go through the evaluation process, only the ones that make it through all stages of screening and due diligence to reach the bottom of the funnel get funding.

The process begins with a start-up applying to the angel group or fund online. In the last several years, software has evolved to allow the pre-screening process to happen through questions asked on the application. Angel groups have criteria that must be met before they look at a company. Every group is slightly different, but typically included are the amount of revenue to date, the structure of the company, and the type of industry.

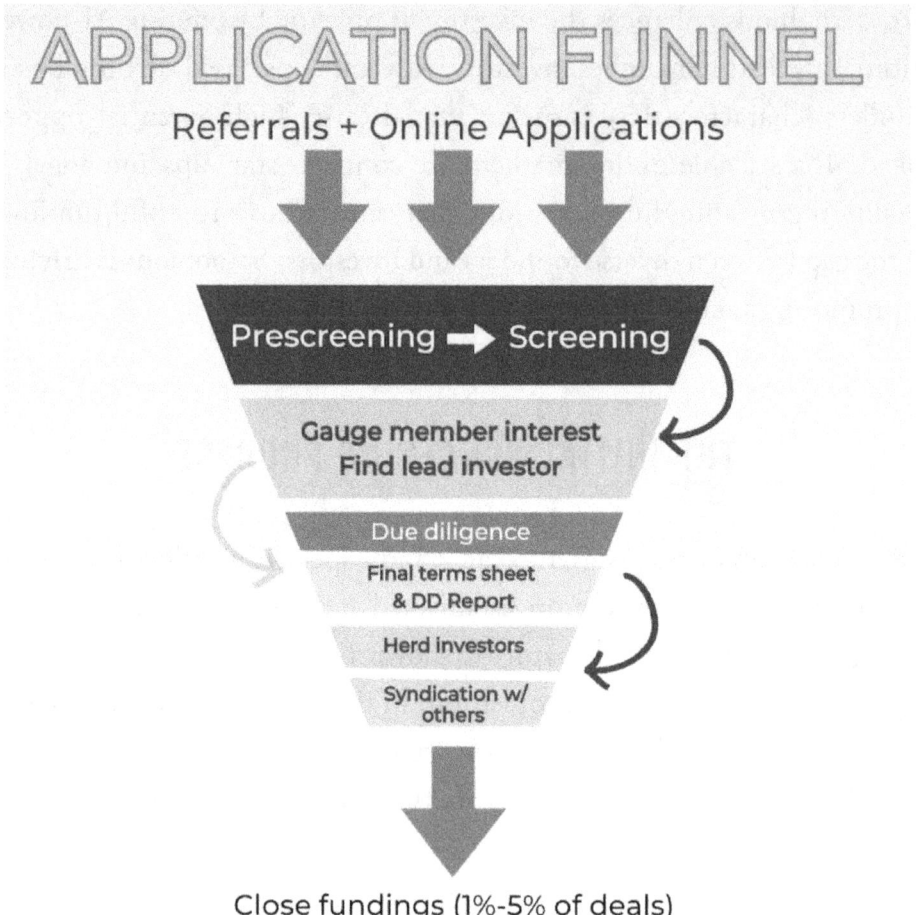

We will use the information from two companies to simulate the screening process. First I'll show you, and then you will have the opportunity to do one yourself. By the time you are done working through this section, you will have some tools to know how to screen a company and what to look for in the due diligence process. However, I do not recommend investing in companies as a solo angel, especially in the beginning. Due diligence is a process that is best done with a diverse group of people with different backgrounds who can help evaluate the opportunity from multiple angles. Plus, the process is more fun and manageable when multiple people help. That is why angels tend to invest through angel groups or a fund where more people can participate in the due diligence process. For those seeking to deepen their due diligence knowledge, the Angel Capital Association offers specialized courses tailored to this complex undertaking.

EVALUATE WITH YOUR HALO NAVIGATOR™

Regardless of the type of company you are looking at, a standard set of questions can be used to make sure you are getting a holistic picture of where the company is now and where they plan to go in the future.

I use the ten questions below when evaluating a company. Most start-ups create what we call a "pitch deck," which is a slide deck outlining the details of the company and the opportunity, or "offering," to invest. The answers to these questions should be found in the company's pitch deck.

- What is the problem being solved?
- What is the solution to the problem? Unique competitive advantage?
- Who has the problem (i.e., who is the target client base and market opportunity)?
- What is the current solution being used without this company? Who are the competitors?
- How will the product or service be marketed and sold?
- How will the company make money?
- Who makes up the team that creates and executes the product or service?
- How much money is being raised now? In the future? How much, if any, was raised before?
- How will investors make a return?
- Why should angels invest?

On the next page is a copy of the questions in a format you can use right here in the workbook. More copies are located at the back of this workbook.

Halo Navigator™ Worksheet

1. What is the problem being solved?

2. What is the solution to the problem? Unique competitive advantage?

3. Who has the problem (i.e., who is the target client base and market opportunity)?

4. What is the current solution being used without this company? Who are the competitors?

5. How will the product or services be marketed and sold?

6. How will the company make money?

7. Who makes up the team that creates and executes the product or services?

8. How much money is being raised now? In the future? How much, if any was raised before?

9. How will investors make a return?

10. Why should angels invest?

Angel groups and angel funds will likely have a screening committee that evaluates the "deal flow" or list of companies applying for funding. If these questions are answered in such a way that sparks a further look, the company moves to the next phase, where all the angel group members review the company, and investment interest is gauged. The process of figuring out who might invest is informal. Some groups raise their hands if they are in a live meeting or email/ballots can be used. With a fund, the fund managers typically get together to look at all the initial details. If there is a certain level of interest, then a deeper dive due diligence begins.

At this point, evaluating a company using these questions could seem daunting. However, reviewing a few examples can demystify the process, making it less intimidating. You might even identify reasons for a swift rejection. Remember, a quick decision of "no" could be because the company doesn't align with your "why" that you identified in Part I of this workbook—and that's OK. Providing a prompt and decisive "no" to an entrepreneur is more beneficial than dragging out the evaluation process for weeks or months only to arrive at the same conclusion later.

PITCH DECK CRITIQUE

Let's imagine an entrepreneur has reached out and would like to set up a meeting. Before taking the meeting, we want to review the pitch deck to see if it fits into our Halo Strategy™ and if we believe the company has potential for growth. Over the next several pages, we will review two different pitch decks. For the first one, I will show each slide with some information and questions I would want to ask the founder after my initial screening. The companies are real and were kind enough to allow me to use some of their information and critique it. I have hidden, changed, or removed proprietary, confidential, or forward-looking information from the decks. This exercise is strictly for educational purposes, and the information is incomplete so could not be used to evaluate the companies. However, in this simulation, I will explain what you should look for in a start-up pitch, even when information on these slides is missing or different. Remember that a pitch deck is designed to entice the potential investor to want to learn more, not to make a decision yet. This is just an initial screening where we want to make notes on what else we want to know should we decide to investigate further (e.g., move the company into a deeper due diligence assessment).

Then, you will have an opportunity to review the second pitch deck on your own and make notes and questions. Once you finish, you will see the same set of slides again, with my notes and questions added to compare. There are no right or wrong answers—you will likely find something I might not have mentioned and vice versa. This is another example of why accessing investment options in collaboration with others can be very helpful.

Let's dive in!

Company One is Bublish—an AI-technology publishing platform to help self-published authors with positioning, marketing, branding, and discoverability.

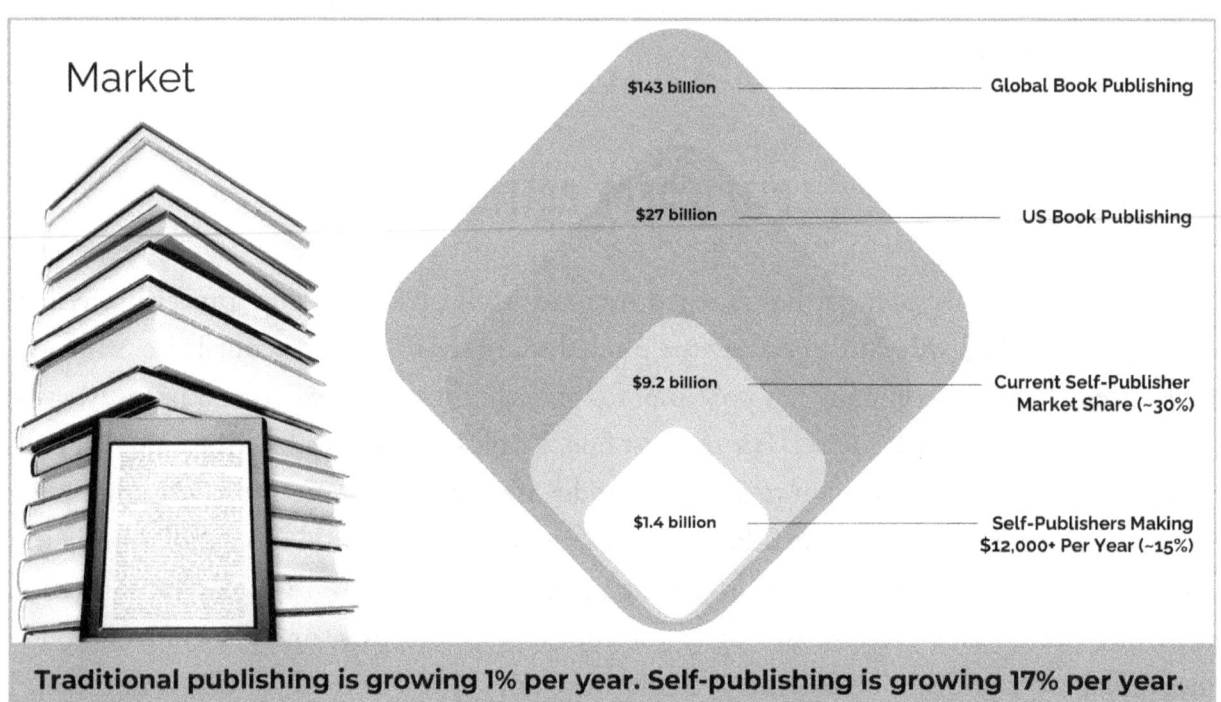

Each pitch deck may present topics in a slightly different order. In this case, Slide 1 shows the size of the market. Understanding the market is crucial, particularly in ensuring it is sufficiently large. This is because a start-up typically only captures a small percentage of the "total addressable market" (TAM). Gaining a deep insight into the TAM helps assess the business's potential scale and viability. Normally, I would not suggest an entrepreneur open with the TAM, but in this case, it is important context for understanding the problem statement on Slide 2. I'm intrigued by the statistics listed at the bottom comparing the traditional publishing market to self-publishing. So, I went to my favorite search engine and did some fact-checking. I found the source and verified the data within one to two minutes. Fact-checking is a good practice throughout the diligence process.

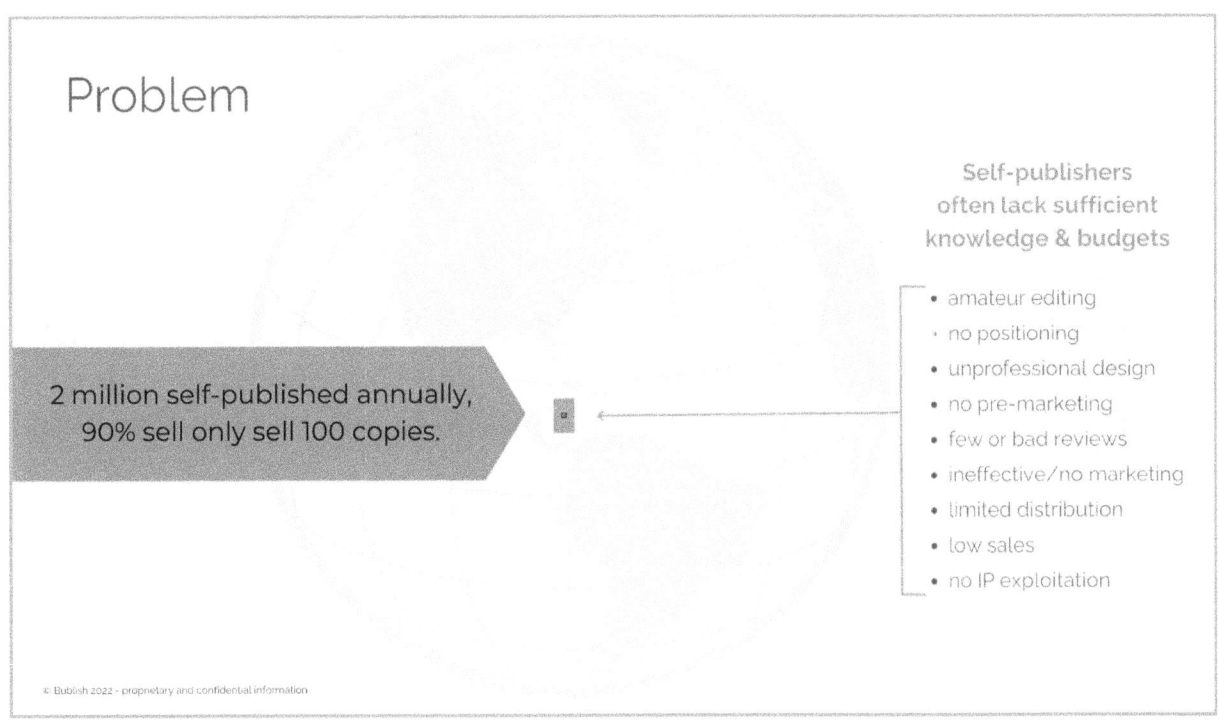

Slide 2 focuses on identifying the problem being solved by the business, which is arguably one of the most crucial aspects of the presentation. If the problem isn't significant or relevant to investors, the entrepreneur risks losing their attention early in the pitch. In essence, if investors aren't convinced of the problem's importance, they may begin to disengage, possibly thinking about their dinner plans rather than the presentation. Therefore, it's vital that the problem is clearly articulated in simple terms, making it easy for investors of all backgrounds to grasp and appreciate its significance. If you don't easily understand the problem statement, be sure to ask questions to get the clarification you need.

Slides 3 and 4 show the solution(s) the company has developed or is developing. In some cases, the solutions are live already, and some are coming soon. Entrepreneurs try to show investors the whole picture of what they are building, not just what has been built so far. I'm interested in learning more about the four Bublish authors who have sold 10,000-plus books and how Bublish helped them do that.

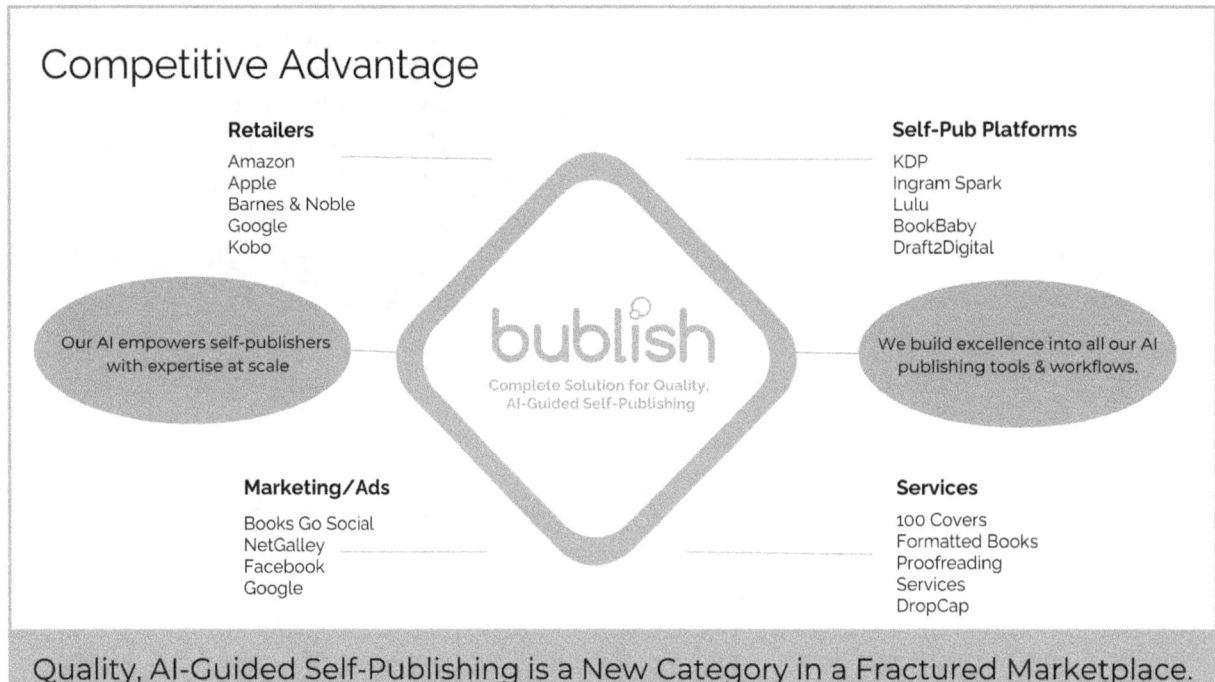

Every start-up should have a good understanding of the competition. Some competitors can be large companies, sometimes smaller companies, or even other start-ups. Investors want to see that the founder/CEO and team have a good understanding of all the ways others are solving the same problem. Red flag: If a company claims it has no competition, it's likely overlooking something. Unless the problem is entirely novel, there is usually some form of existing solution, even if it's not ideal. Alternatively, this could indicate that there is no market demand for what they are creating.

When ride-sharing companies first came on the scene, they may have said they didn't have competition because nothing like this existed where a person would pick you up in their own car. But in fact, taxis were the competition. In this case, the problem—transportation—did have a solution: the taxi. But the ride-sharing companies had an improved solution. Another example is that an entrepreneur may invent a unique product to solve multiple problems, yet each problem was previously addressed by different solutions. Therefore, the new solution must be very compelling to sway users to switch their behavior.

The team slide serves as a crucial indicator of the company's organizational structure and how built out the team is at this stage in their early life. While I've omitted names and photos here, the positions are outlined in the top row, and in this case, advisors and board members are listed in the second row. It's common for entrepreneurs to include future team prospects as well, especially if part of the reason they are raising money is to hire. Seeing a team of at least six, as on this slide, with multiple advisors and board members, is a good indicator the CEO has surrounded themselves with a team positioned for growth. But this would be something to dig into more in a deeper dive once the company is through the initial screening. A solo founder with no other team members is a red flag, suggesting that the company is still in its very early stages, and could be a higher-risk investment. Additionally, if team members are only working part-time or juggling other jobs, it may indicate lack of commitment to the new venture especially if they haven't yet left their previous jobs.

Product Strategy

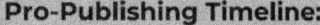

Pro-Publishing Timeline:
Create an innovative user experience that guides authors through an AI-automated, professional publishing process.

AI Tools & Features:
Revamp publishing workflows with AI and automation to reduce costs, raise quality & improve outcomes at SCALE.

Subscription Pricing:
Offer tiered subscription to lower cost of publishing quality books while improving operating efficiencies and profitability

Quality AI-Guided Self-Publishing

We're using artificial intelligence to help authors self-publish better books and market them more effectively so they can sell thousands of copies, instead of hundreds.

AI combined with our proven self-publishing process empowers authors to achieve better results for fraction of the cost.

After covering the problem, solution, competition, market, and team, we can dig deeper into the product, revenue generation, and business plan. This slide highlights the key features and the company's revenue model, with a focus on a subscription-based pricing strategy. This approach supports the primary goal of delivering quality AI-guided self-publishing services. Investors are typically drawn to start-ups with subscription-based revenue streams because, while customers can cancel, valuable products that do an excellent job delivering benefits to their customers often retain customers for months or even years. This means the company benefits from recurring revenue, reducing the need to acquire new customers constantly.

Pro-Publishing Timeline

Quality AI-Guided Self-Publishing

Innovative user experience guides authors through an automated, professional publishing process.

Positioning & Planning Studio → Writing & Editing Studio → Design & Production Studio → Distribution Studio → Marketing Studio

Shared Data & AI Logic

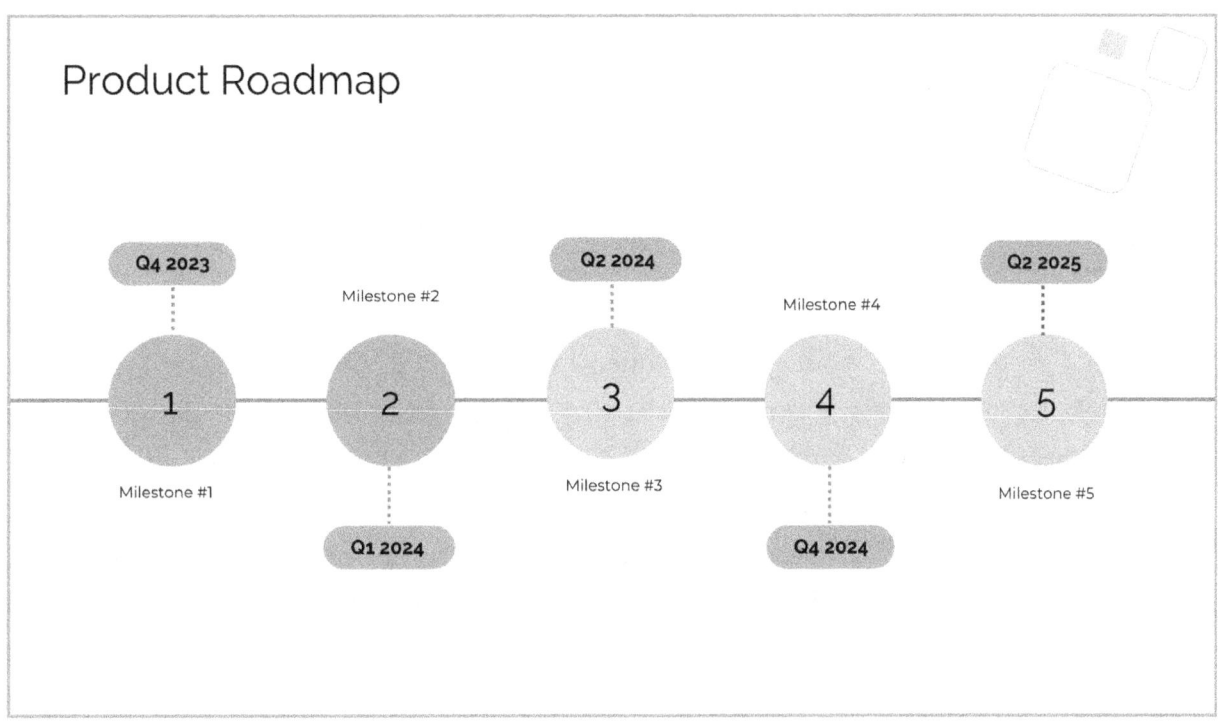

Product Roadmap

- Q4 2023 — 1 — Milestone #1
- Milestone #2 — 2 — Q1 2024
- Q2 2024 — 3 — Milestone #3
- Milestone #4 — 4 — Q4 2024
- Q2 2025 — 5 — Milestone #5

After addressing the company's product and revenue generation strategy, we can now examine the timeline detailing how these plans will unfold. These two slides provide additional insights into what the customer will receive and the development of the end product over time. At this stage, I would request a demo from the CEO to gain a comprehensive understanding of the product and its functionality, which is crucial for meeting the goal of authors who want to sell more than 10,000 books.

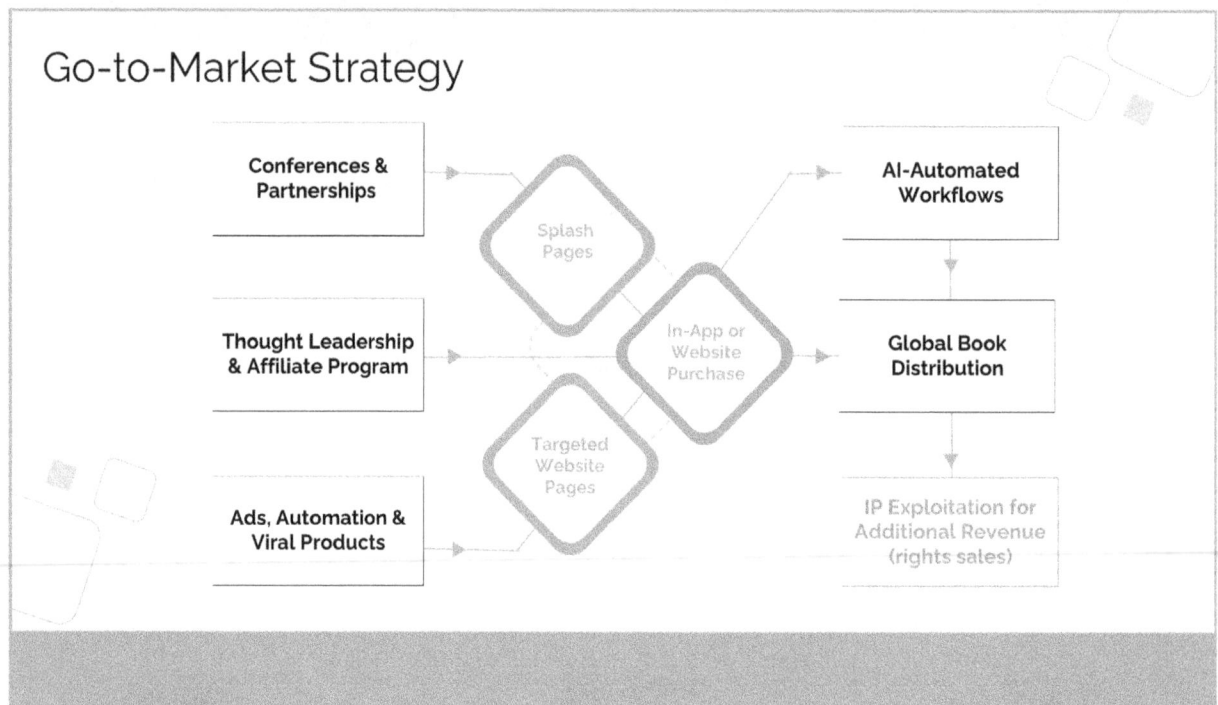

The term "go-to-market strategy" is frequently mentioned in angel investing circles. Essentially, it refers to how a company plans to acquire customers and begin generating revenue. It's crucial to assess whether this strategy is realistic and viable. At this point, I would inquire about the CEO's industry connections and expertise to successfully bring their product to market. Additionally, I would ask how many customers they have currently, how many of those customers have beta-tested the product, and the company's timeline and cost projections for achieving market scalability.

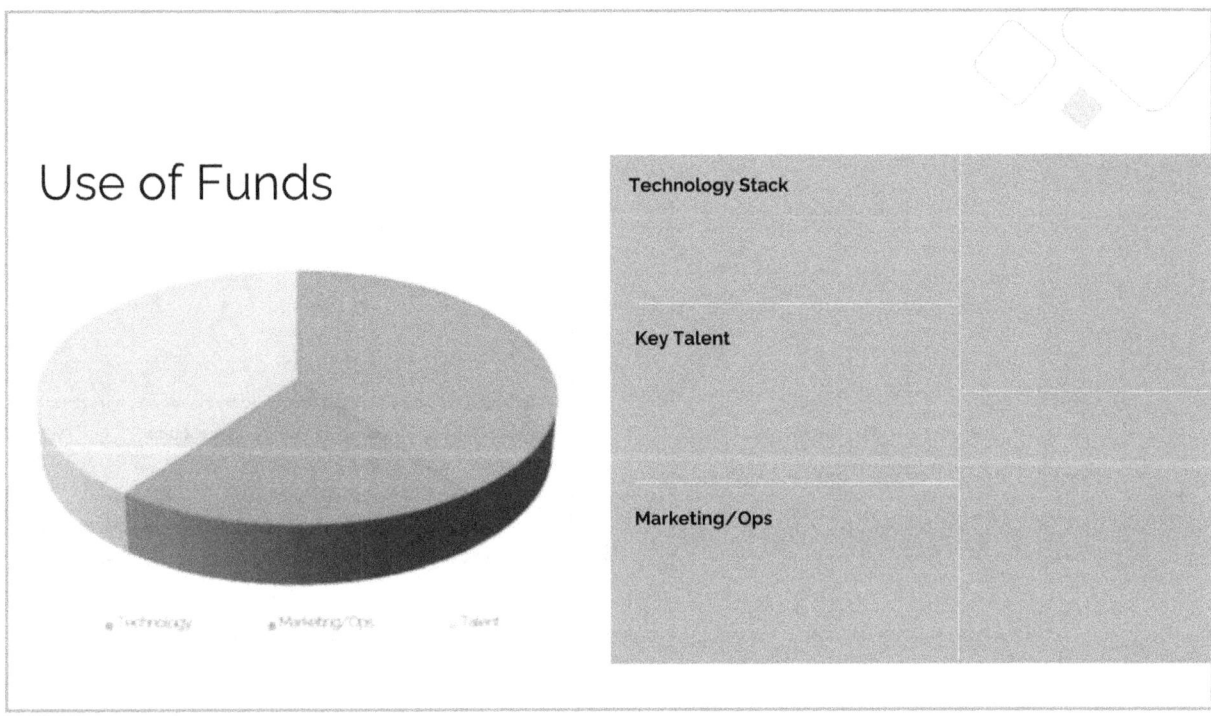

Here is an example of what a "Use of Funds" slide would look like. This slide typically details the offering, including the amount of money the company is raising, and the valuation at which investors can buy in. The company's valuation is usually negotiated between the CEO and the lead investor, who often contributes the most capital. This slide will also outline how the raised funds will be allocated. In this example, even though you don't see specific figures, you can see that the funds would be used in three areas: technology development, hiring, and marketing/operations.

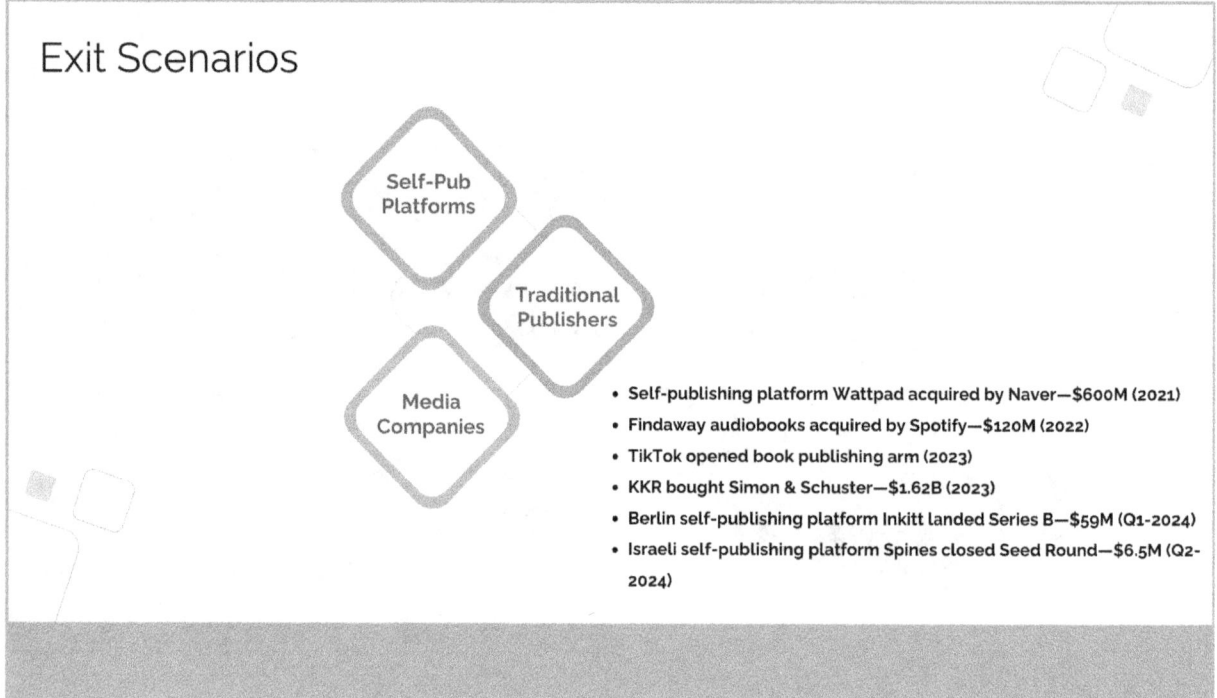

The exit scenario is of particular interest to investors as it outlines potential pathways to achieve returns on their investment. Unlike public stocks, investing in a start-up is not a liquid asset; you cannot sell your interest at any time to retrieve your money. Instead, you must wait for a liquidity event such as an acquisition (the most common path) or an initial public offering (IPO) (a rare path for only a small fraction of highly successful start-ups). This slide highlights two key aspects: the potential acquisition avenues for the company and examples of similar companies in the industry that have been acquired, including their acquisition prices. Here would be another place to do some fact-checking. In less than three seconds, I found information on Spotify's acquisition of Findaway Audiobook. Keep in mind—past performance is never an indicator of future performance, so just because a company in the same space was acquired for a specific price in a certain time doesn't mean that will happen to another company.

Every pitch deck should conclude with a wrap-up slide featuring the CEO's contact information, ensuring it's easy to locate. Additionally, some start-ups include a summary slide at the end highlighting key reasons investors should be enthusiastic about the opportunity and consider investing.

YOUR OPPORTUNITY TO REVIEW A START-UP

Activity: Now it is your turn to review the pitch deck of a start-up. On the next several pages you will find the pitch deck of Really Good Boxed Wine, a company dedicated to crafting exceptional wines while improving sustainability—reducing packaging by more than 50%, cutting down on shipping costs, and minimizing carbon footprint. Take some time to review each slide and make notes and questions in the space provided. Even without seeing the redacted information, you can still mark down the questions you would have for the CEO. Refer to your Halo Navigator™ when needed. After you review this deck, you will see my notes and the questions I would ask. Keep in mind, our thoughts and questions may be different and that's OK as it illustrates the value of involving multiple people in any assessment.

UNDERSTAND HOW TO FIND AND EVALUATE DEALS

ADDRESSING THE CHALLENGES OF THE MODERN WINE INDUSTRY

A critical need exists to **attract new wine drinkers** while continuing to **appeal to key consumer base.**

INNOVATION
Resistance to adapt to the changing market has contributed to annual declining sales and an aging core customer.
*Only 1 in 5 Millennial and Gen Z drinkers choose wine as top beverage choice.

MODERATION
+**51% of US drinkers are now practicing moderate consumption**, driving sales to spirits and beer, which are easier to enjoy in small quantities vs. bottled wine, that has to be quickly finished once open.

SUSTAINABILITY
78% of Americans cite sustainability as a factor in purchase choice. **Glass bottles contribute **51% of the industry's carbon footprint**, yet remain the primary packaging option.

*Statista, Sept. 2023
IWSR, Apr. 2023
**CA Sustainable Wine Alliance, 2022

YEARS OF CONSISTENT TRENDS SHOW A PATH TO SUCCESS

The outlook remains positive within specific categories most desired by today's consumer.

FORMAT
The ONLY format with growing market share is boxed wine.
Super-premium boxed wine brands (>$20 3L) are seeing an outsized 17.3% YOY Sales increase.

PREMIUMIZATION
$15-$20/750ml category has recorded 10+ years of continuous growth.
Value price categories have declined 21% in sales volume over this same time period.

QUALITY
Consumers spend more, even if drinking less, to ensure better quality and "cleaner" consumption. This has led to growth in wines with fewer additives and lower sugar content.

2022 Growth by Format
- Bottles
- Cans
- >$20 3L BiB: +17.3%

2023 Change in Sales by Price
- <$8
- $8-12
- $12-20: +7.3%

Wine today can contain:
- 60+ Approved Additives
- Up to 220 g/L Sugar

MEET REALLY GOOD BOXED WINE

SIZE
3 Liters (4 standard wine bottles)

QUALITY
Hand-crafted wine, would sell for $30+/bottle

FRESHNESS
Airtight, one-way valve keeps wine fresh for 6 weeks after opening

PRICE
$70 per box ($17.50/bottle)

WINEMAKING
No artificial additives, sustainable, 0g sugar, low sulfites, vegan

PACKAGING
Recyclable kraft box, food-grade/ BPA free bag

RGBW OPERATES IN THE FASTEST GROWING PRICE TIER AND FORMAT OF THE U.S. WINE MARKET

As the industry premiumizes, wine drinkers are embracing the boxed format to save money, drink sustainably, & practice moderation.

+17.3%
Growth of $20+ boxed wines in 2022

9.3%
Boxed wine share of US wine market (vs. 1% for canned wine)

40%
of drinkers under 43 have bought boxed wine in past year

28%
2022 bottled wine sales >$15 per bottle

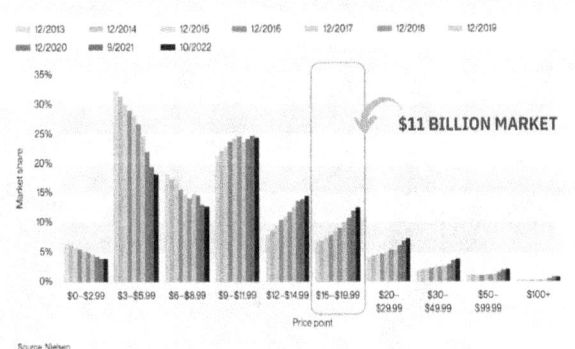

ANNUAL CHANGE IN SHARE (VALUE) BY PRICE POINT

$11 BILLION MARKET

Source: Nielsen

WILL AMERICAN DRINKERS EMBRACE BOXED FINE WINE?

The answer is yes! It's what's inside that counts, and we even *wow* the skeptics.

| Sales | Data | Goes Here |

UNDERSTAND HOW TO FIND AND EVALUATE DEALS

BRAND SENTIMENT

Both wine industry thought-leaders and RGBW customers give us consistently strong reviews

Excellent!

One believes the wine that they drink is pretty good until they try Really Good Boxed Wine!! I am a wine drinker and the difference is amazing and the price actually ends up being less expensive because you get four bottles in a box!! Highly highly recommend!! There is nothing like it on the market.

Highly recommended!

Very well made, if I didn't see it poured from the box I would have guessed it was poured from a $30-40 bottle. I ordered another box to have ready when my family comes for Thanksgiving!

1000+ Verified Reviews

"It's aptly named and is a rock-solid, satisfying boxed wine...it's a terrific value."

JEB DUNNUCK
JebDunnuck.com

This is INDEED, "Really Good Boxed Wine".

MATT KETTMANN,
Wine Enthusiast

...the company name says it all...the quality is sound.

KEITH BEAVERS,
VinePair

OUR POSITION AS THE CATEGORY LEADER

Increased options of higher priced boxed wine has improved category acceptance, yet we remain the ONLY winery offering the quality of fine wine, a diverse selection, and National availability.

	Price per 3L	Vintage	Varietal	Sub-AVA	Availability
Competitor 1	$160	Yes	Yes	Yes	No
Competitor 2	$95	Yes	Yes	Yes	No
Competitor 3	$89	No	No	No	Yes
Really Good Boxed Wine	$70	Yes	Yes	Yes	Yes
Competitor 4	$70	Yes	Yes	No	Yes
Competitor 5	$55	No	No	No	Yes
Competitor 6	$50	No	No	No	Yes
Competitor 7	$50	No	No	No	Yes

*Mailing List Only

OUR TARGET CUSTOMER

RGBW is proving to be broadly appealing across age, gender, and region.
However, we have a disproportionate right to win with two key consumer segments:

WINE KNOWLEGABLE YOUNG PROFESSIONALS

Cares about experiences, authenticity, quality at a value, sustainability, and freedom to be unique. Grew up online, frequent early adopter.

- Age 30-45 w/ above avg. income
- Frequently spends $15+/bottle
- Consider themselves wine drinkers and pride themselves on drinking good wine

RETIRED WINE DRINKERS

Relaxed lifestyle that allows for indulgence in the finer things, but making lifestyle adjustments. Loyal to brands that deliver consistent quality.

- Age 65+, comfortably retired
- Deeper understanding of fine wine
- Places high value on quality, authenticity, and rich experiences in wine

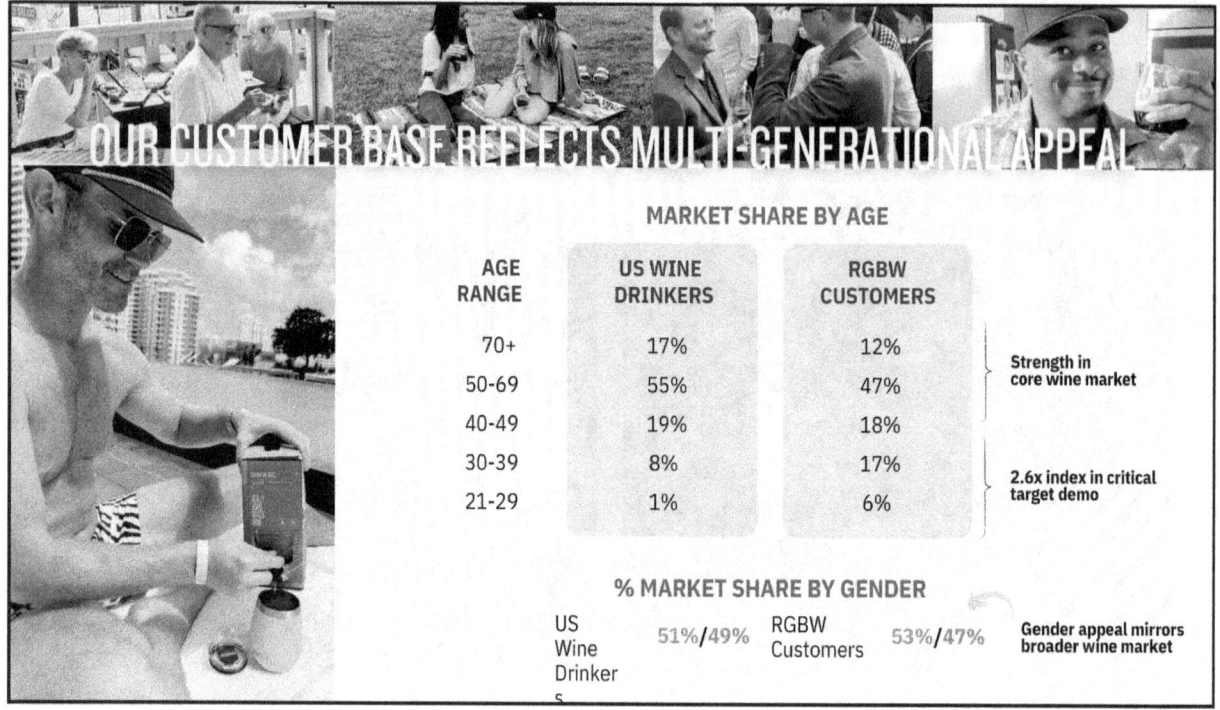

A BUSINESS PREPARED TO ACCELERATE GROWTH

FINANCIAL IMPROVEMENTS VS. YEAR 1

Avg. Monthly Revenue
Gross Margin
Contribution Margin
Net Margin
AOV

CORE CUSTOMER METRICS

LTV
Repeat Purchase Rate
Wine Club ARR
Wholesale Markets
Account Reorder Rate

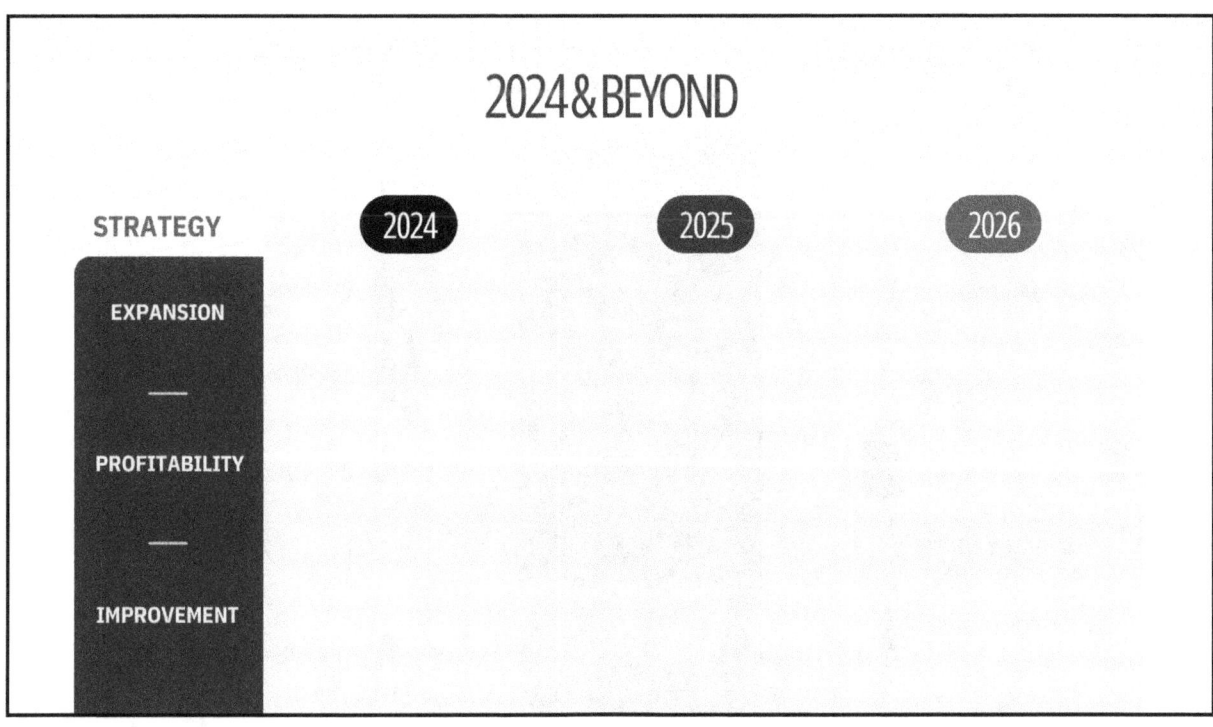

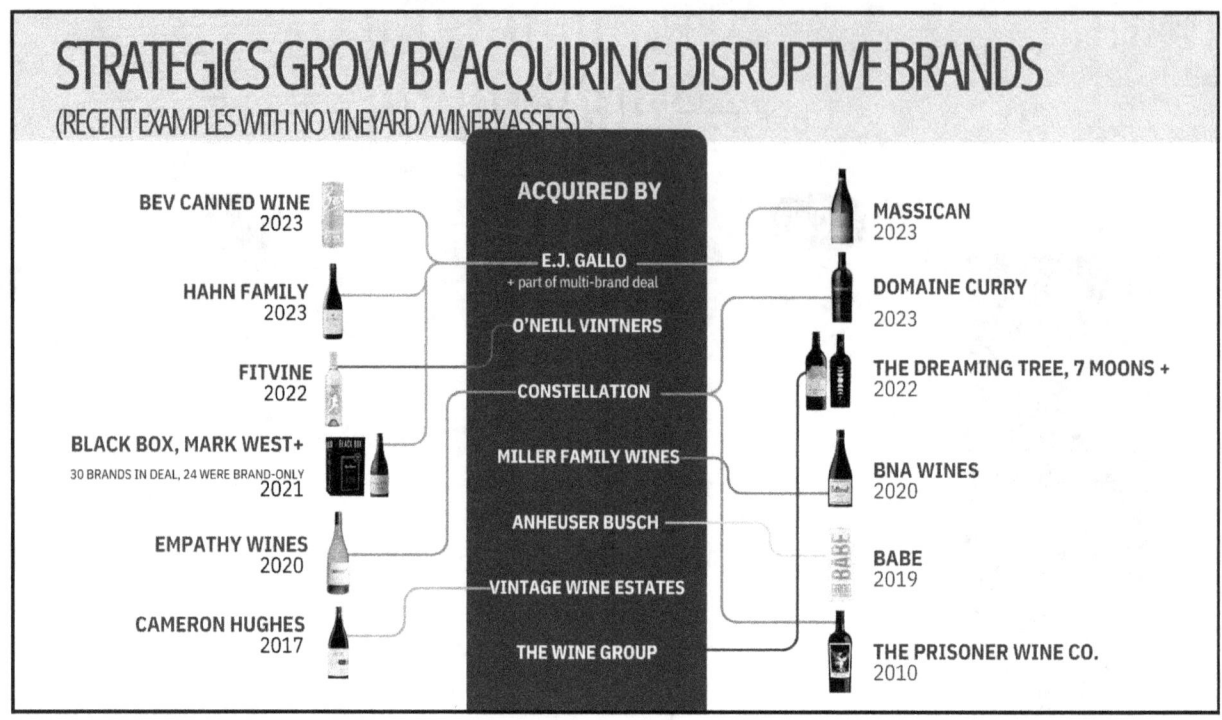

AND CATEGORY-DEFINING BEVALC BRANDS CAN EXIT AT 10-20X REVENUE

DIAGEO

ACQUISITION
- CASAMIGOS *20X*
- CASAMIGOS
- PELIGROSO
- SPIRITS
- DON JULIO
- DELEON
- UNITED NATIONAL
- BELSAZAR
- PIERDE ALMAS
- SICHUAN CHENGDU
- SHUIJINGFANG
- GROUP
- AVIATION *15X*
- TRUPPLESWORTH

INVESTMENT
- STAUNING
- WHISKEY
- STARWARD WHISKY
- SEEDLIP (ACQUIRED)

Pernod Ricard

ACQUISITION
- KENWOOD
- MONKEY 47
- DEL MAGUEY
- AVION
- SMOOTH AMBLER
- CASTLE BRANDS
- MALFY GIN
- RABBITS FOOT

Constellation Brands

ACQUISITION
- DUNKY BUDDHA
- SCHRADER CELLARS
- BARDSTOWN
- HIGH WEST
- PRISONER
- BALLAST POINT
- MELODY WINES
- EMPATHY WINES *10X*
- CASA NOBLE

INVESTMENT
- AUSTINCOCKTAILS
- VIVIFY
- DURHAM
- MONTANA
- NELSON'S GREEN
- BRIAR
- EL SILENCIO
- BLACK BUTTON
- CRAFTHOUSE

BACARDI

ACQUISITION
- BANKS
- PATRON SPIRITS
- LEBLON
- STILLHOUSE
- ANGEL'S ENVY *12X*

INVESTMENT
- ILLEGAL
- TEELING
- COMPASS BOX

Beam Suntory

ACQUISITION
- SIPSMITH

INVESTMENT
- BARTESIAN
- ABV BRANDS

BROWN-FORMAN

ACQUISITION
- ENRICH
- STONE CASTLE
- IRISH WHISKEY

ABInBev

ACQUISITION
- CUTWATER SPIRITS *12X*
- SPIKED SELTZER

INVESTMENT
- KOMBREWCHA
- SATURDAY
- SESSION
- ELECTRIC SKY
- CANVAS
- ATOM GROUP
- GOLIVE
- PORTES
- SABSE ROSE
- POUP MOUNTAIN
- SWITCHED

MOLSON COORS

ACQUISITION
- CLEARLY KOMBUCHA

INVESTMENT
- BHAKTI CHAI

Now that you have had the chance to do your initial screening of Really Good Boxed Wine—see my notes and the questions I would ask in the next several pages.

Right away I'm intrigued by the cover slide. I can see the product. The packaging looks different than other wines or even boxed wines I've seen before—it is skinny.

This slide shows the problem they are working to solve, and the comment about glass bottles significantly contributing to the industry's carbon footprint caught my attention. It's something I hadn't considered before. Why must wine predominantly be packaged in 750-milliliter glass bottles? It's another example of doing things a certain way simply because that's how they've always been done. Given the evolving preferences of the younger generation and the inefficiencies in packaging, this industry seems ripe for disruption.

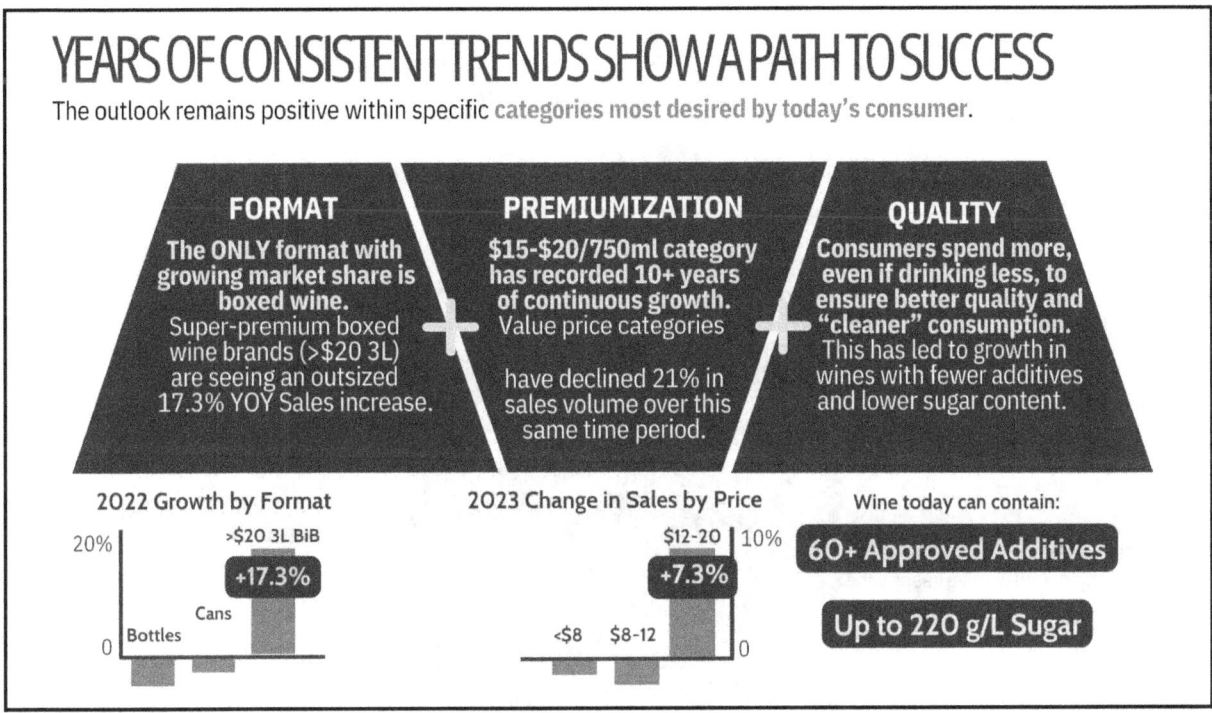

This slide continues to outline the problem. I would want to verify some of the statistics presented such as the claim that "the only format with growing market share is boxed wine." Additionally, I'm not familiar with the price sensitivity in the alcohol category, so I would need to conduct further research in that area as well.

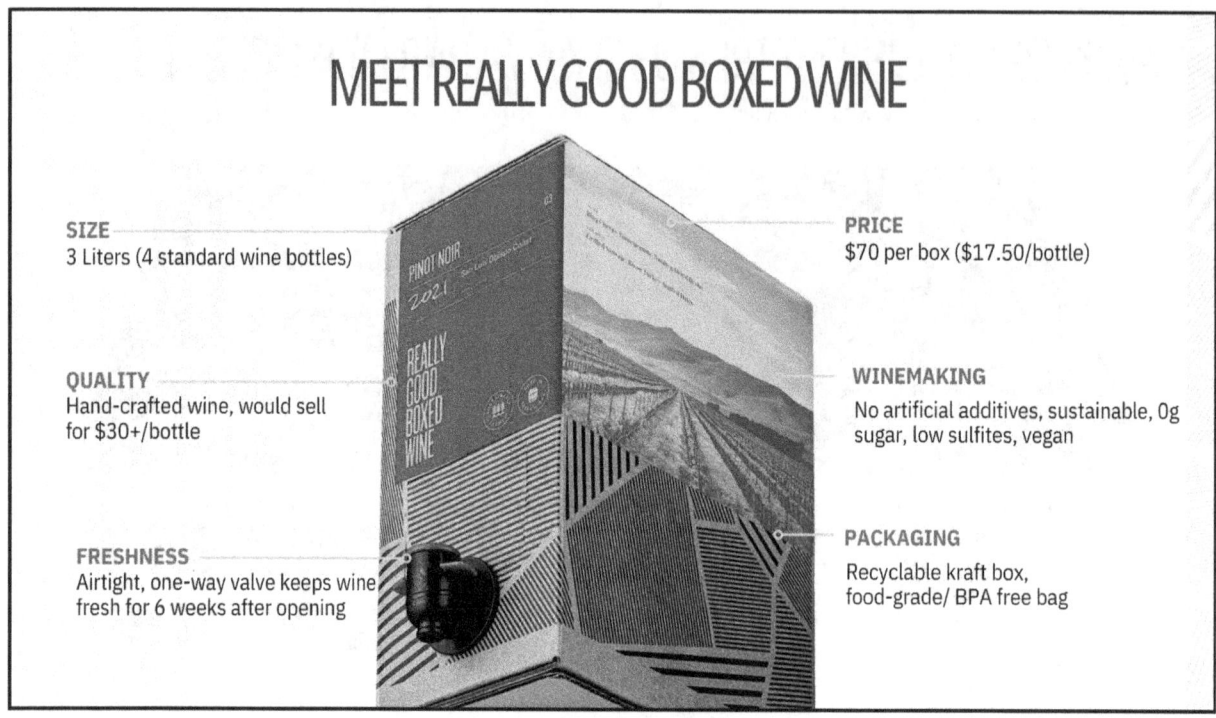

Here is the solution: Really Good Boxed Wine. It's impressive that this box can hold the equivalent of four standard bottles and keep the wine fresh for up to six weeks. I appreciate that the bag is BPA-free. Additionally, the price is attractive for boxed wine, especially considering it features a specific grape (Pinot Noir) and a vintage (2021), which seems uncommon from my limited knowledge of boxed wine, yet is an important characteristic for high-quality wine.

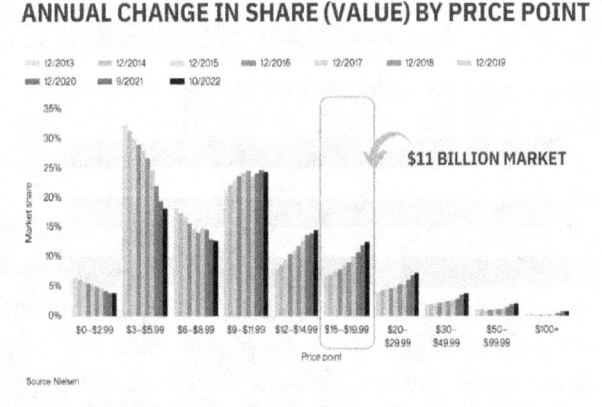

This slide provides valuable market insights for potential investors. The statistics presented about the industry are intriguing and warrant further investigation. As you can see, evaluating a company for investment involves not only understanding the company itself, but also gaining insights into the broader market. For instance, I was surprised to learn that boxed wine accounts for more than 9 percent of all wine purchases in the US.

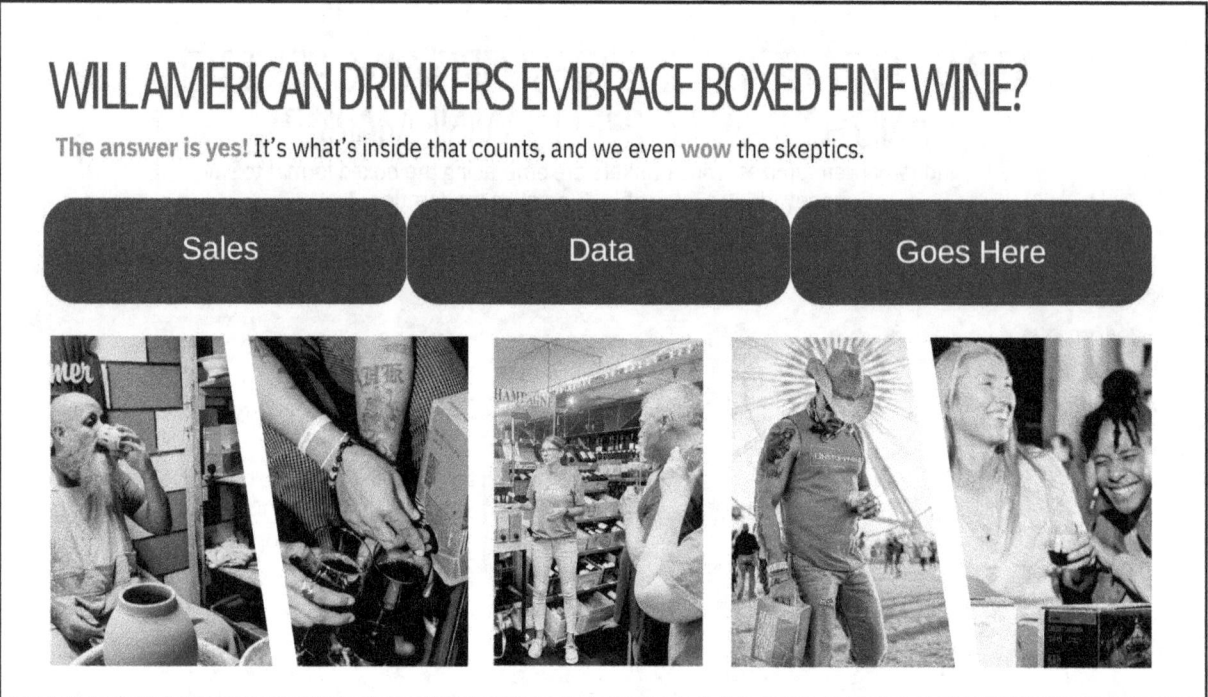

Boxed fine wine? At first glance, those words seem contradictory. This is where I'd look deeper, asking the management team about their customer discovery process, feedback, and reviews. Additionally, I would want to speak directly with actual customers to gauge their experiences. It's also an ideal time to use your favorite search engine to look up reviews of Really Good Boxed Wine online.

Great, here are some reviews provided by the company. In the previous slide, I suggested I would want to research to find additional reviews. In an evaluation, I would then compare the reviews discovered with the ones presented by the company to see if they align.

OUR POSITION AS THE CATEGORY LEADER

Increased options of higher priced boxed wine has improved category acceptance, yet we remain the ONLY winery offering the quality of fine wine, a diverse selection, and National availability.

	Price per 3L	Vintage	Varietal	Sub-AVA	Availability
Competitor 1	$160	Yes	Yes	Yes	No
Competitor 2	$95	Yes	Yes	Yes	No
Competitor 3	$89	No	No	No	Yes
Really Good Boxed Wine	$70	Yes	Yes	Yes	Yes
Competitor 4	$70	Yes	Yes	No	Yes
Competitor 5	$55	No	No	No	Yes
Competitor 6	$50	No	No	No	Yes
Competitor 7	$50	No	No	No	Yes

*Mailing List Only

This is the competition slide. It highlights other boxed wines sold in the same volume—3 liters or four standard bottles. The comparison includes price, vintage, and varietal information. Since I'm not a wine industry expert, I'm unsure what "sub-AVA" means, so I'll need to ask the team and suggest they add a definition to the slide. As part of the screening process, I would conduct an online search for boxed wines to identify any potential competitors not listed here that I would want to discuss with the company.

OUR TARGET CUSTOMER

RGBW is proving to be broadly appealing across age, gender, and region. However, we have a disproportionate right to win with two key consumer segments:

WINE KNOWLEGABLE YOUNG PROFESSIONALS

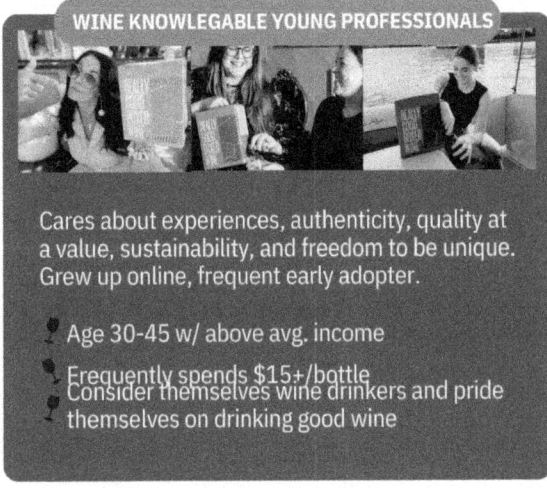

Cares about experiences, authenticity, quality at a value, sustainability, and freedom to be unique. Grew up online, frequent early adopter.

- Age 30-45 w/ above avg. income
- Frequently spends $15+/bottle
- Consider themselves wine drinkers and pride themselves on drinking good wine

RETIRED WINE DRINKERS

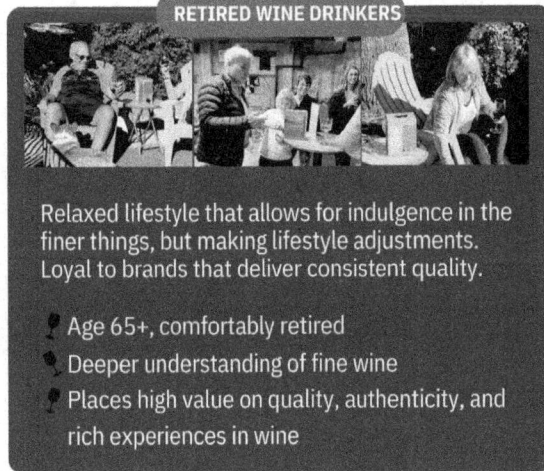

Relaxed lifestyle that allows for indulgence in the finer things, but making lifestyle adjustments. Loyal to brands that deliver consistent quality.

- Age 65+, comfortably retired
- Deeper understanding of fine wine
- Places high value on quality, authenticity, and rich experiences in wine

I appreciate that the company has identified specific target customers who align with its ideal demographic. While many people drink wine, and Really Good Boxed Wine could aim to reach a broad audience, focusing early efforts on pleasing particular segments often leads to greater success for young companies or start-ups. The two target audiences they've chosen seem logical, but I would still want to conduct further research by talking to customers and reviewing online feedback to validate these choices.

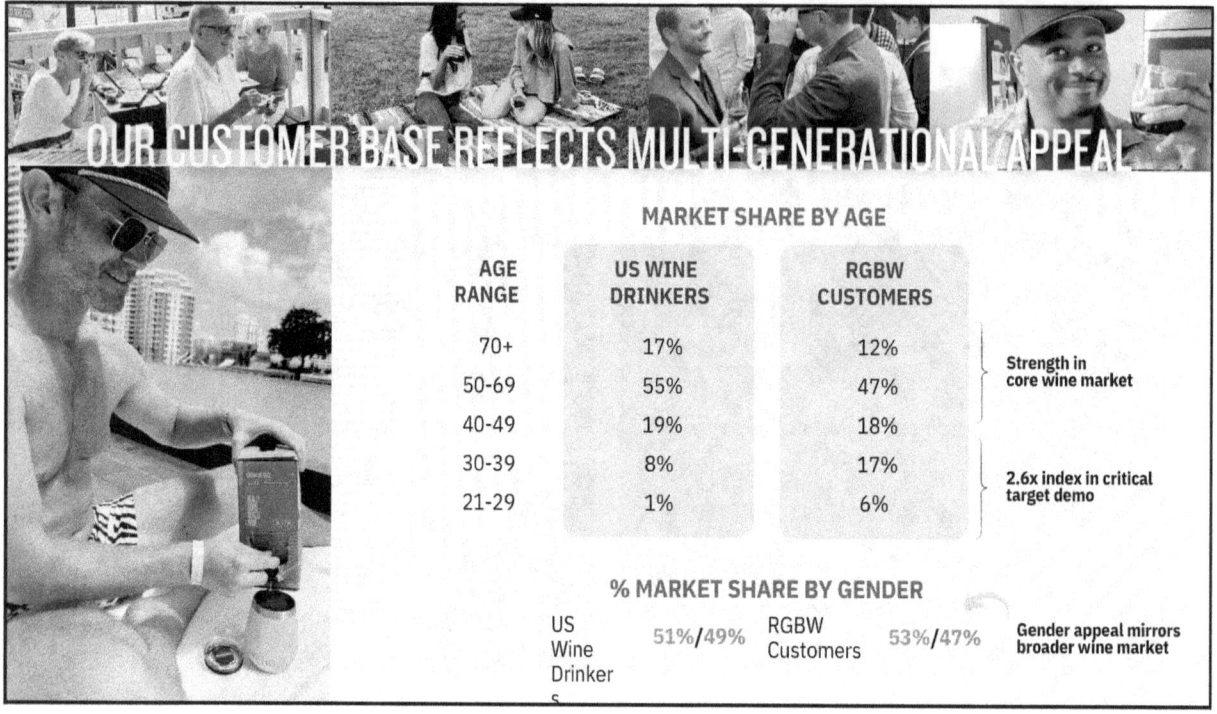

Here are additional intriguing statistics about the customer base and the wine's appeal across various demographic segments. If I had seen this slide before the previous one, I might have thought the company lacked focus. However, the previous slide clarified their targeted approach, and this slide illustrates potential future expansion once they have established a strong foundation with their initial target demographics and psychographics.

The team slide is currently showing four individuals working on the business. However, there may be additional team members not pictured here. I would also like to learn about their advisors and board of directors. It's encouraging to see a female winemaker, which I have heard is quite rare in the industry.

> ## A BUSINESS PREPARED TO ACCELERATE GROWTH
>
> **FINANCIAL IMPROVEMENTS VS. YEAR 1**
>
> Avg. Monthly Revenue
> Gross Margin
> Contribution Margin
> Net Margin
> AOV
>
> **CORE CUSTOMER METRICS**
>
> LTV
> Repeat Purchase Rate
> Wine Club ARR
> Wholesale Markets
> Account Reorder Rate

This slide would typically display the company's financial information and customer metrics. While I have removed the specific numbers for confidentiality, a slide like this would show an idea of the company's potential financial growth. Investors often look at lifetime value (LTV) for companies offering consumable products, which indicates repeat customers. I'm also interested in learning more about their wine club and its impact on customer spending.

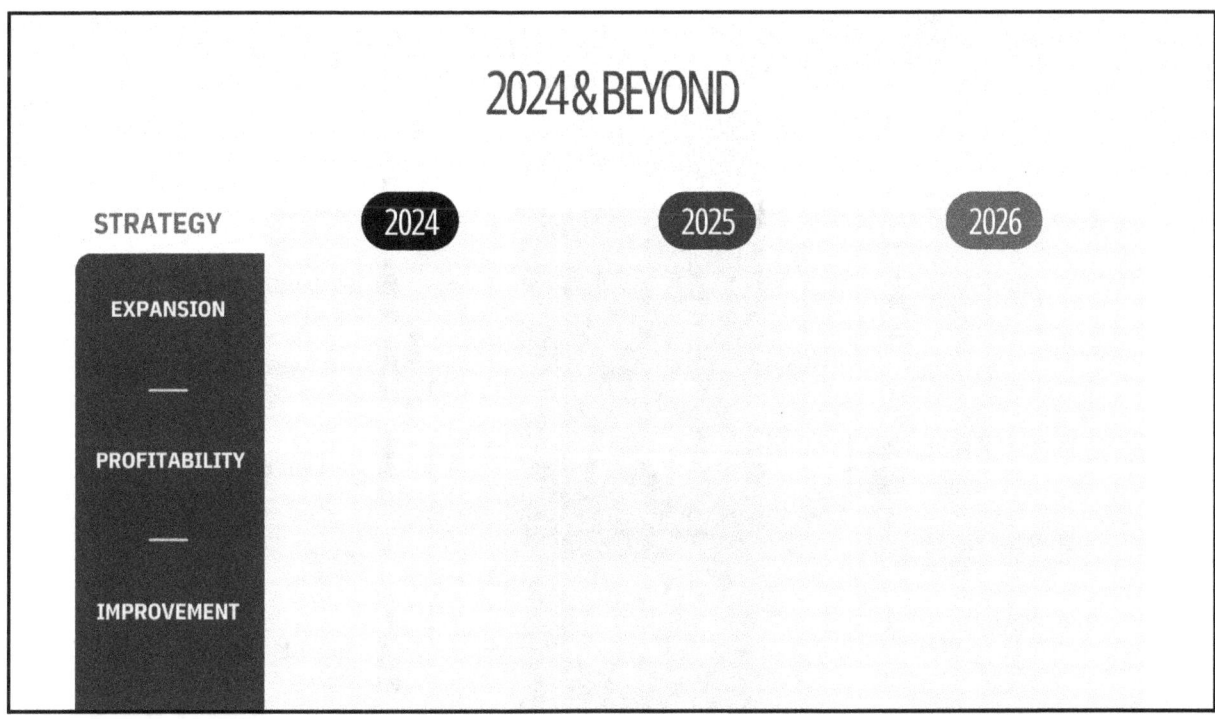

A slide like this would outline the company's plan to expand and grow the business and achieve profitability, meaning when revenues will exceed expenses. Some milestones in any company may require considerable time and effort to accomplish. During the screening process, I would dive deeper with the management team to understand their strategies.

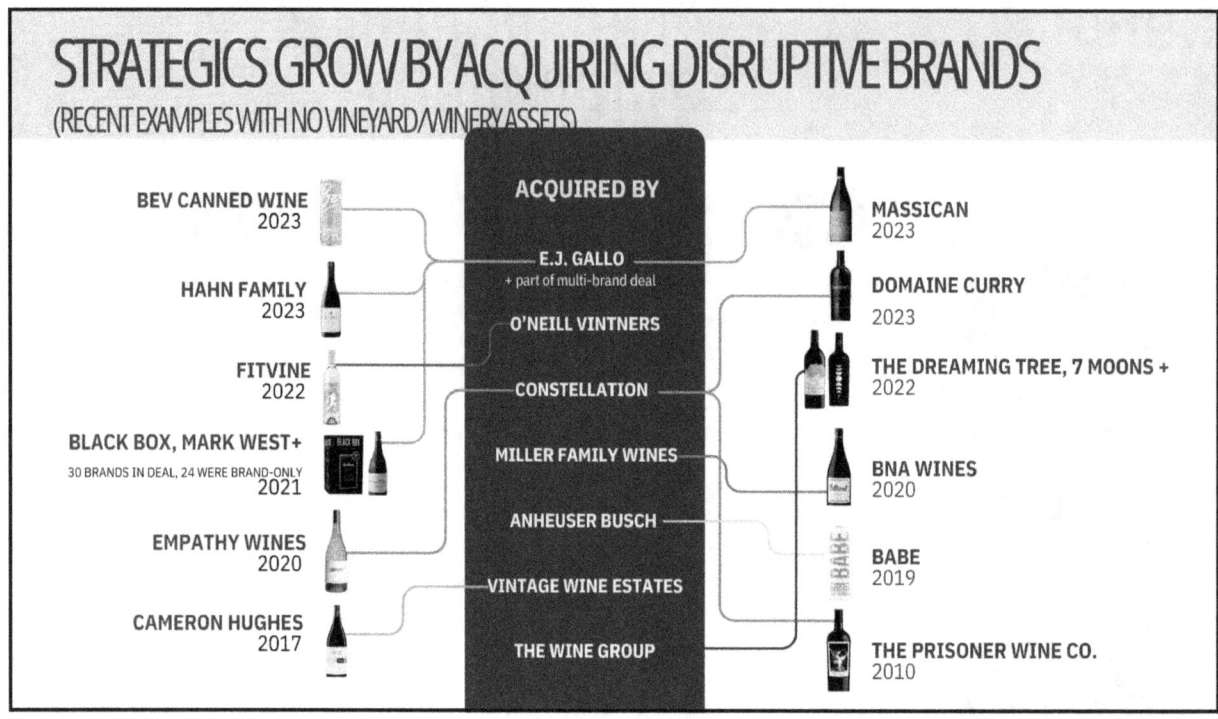

Investors are keen to understand how they will earn a return on their investment, and the most common way for a start-up to achieve a liquidity event or exit that returns capital to investors is through acquisition. This slide illustrates the merger and acquisition (M&A) activity in the alcohol industry. Fact-checking would be good to do here.

In the previous slide, we saw the M&A activity in the alcohol industry. This slide highlights the revenue multiples typically observed during acquisitions. This information requires verification. For example, a 20x revenue multiple suggests that if a company's annual sales are $5 million (hypothetically), its acquisition price could be $100 million.

Typically, the final four or five slides of a pitch deck cover the company's financial projections, the amount of funding sought, the intended use of those funds, and reasons why an investor should be enthusiastic about getting involved. Keep in mind that the timeline and budget presented by the company are often optimistic, so anticipate that scaling the company will likely take at least two to three times longer and cost two to three times more than initially projected. Further investigation could involve running a few scenarios to see how time and cost sensitive their financial projections are.

The closing slide usually has contact information for the CEO, making it easy for investors to reach out. Usually, all members of an angel group and all fund managers see a company's pitch deck. However, one point person who reaches out to the company founder or CEO will keep communication efficient.

AFTER THE PITCH

After the pitch and initial screening, the investors decide if they are interested in possibly investing in the company. If so, due diligence begins. There is a lot to evaluate during this phase, with angel groups usually taking two to three weeks or up to three to six months to work on due diligence for one company. A team forms, and each member of the team picks an area to work on. The main areas to evaluate are:

- The team—Who do they have and need to make this a success?

- The addressable market—Who wants what they are selling?

- The competition—Who else is doing this?

- The product—Does it work? Will people use it?

- The business model—Do or will they make money? Is this a company that can be sold down the road and investors will make money?

- The offering—How much money are they asking for, and what specifically do they plan to do with it?

- The term sheet—if they have one yet—What are the details of what investors can expect to get for their money?

Answering these questions will help you do a deeper dive, and as an activity in Part III, you will use these questions to fill out your Halo Navigator Deeper Dive worksheet. We will not be covering full due diligence in this workbook as that usually involves a group of investors working together to evaluate the company. However, once all the information from a full due diligence is collected from the group, it is gathered in a memo outlining the pros and cons of these areas. For example, maybe the company has a great founder, but the team isn't built out yet. Many angels say it's best to bet on the jockey (i.e., the founder), not the horse (i.e., the product or service being developed); the team is a critical part of the deal.

I've worked on diligence teams that were very organized and some that were not. Either way, participating in several due diligence teams is one of the best ways to learn about angel investing. This can be done within an angel group, or fund managers often encourage LPs to participate in diligence teams, too. The more experienced angels take the lead, and the newer angels help with specific assignments, such as calling a customer to see if they like the product or searching online for some competitors. Fund managers are usually quite experienced and might hire an analyst to help with the diligence work.

Once the diligence memo is finished, angels or fund managers decide whether to invest. You will never know everything to make the perfect decision, but if you do enough diligence, you will know enough to make a decision that works for you.

As the investors in an angel group decide, the group leader or fund manager often talks to other angel groups or funds to see if they are interested. This is called the syndication or deal-sharing process. Angels and fund managers also tend to share due diligence memos. Once all the investors have committed, money is wired to the company, and the deal is closed. In addition to learning through being a part of a due diligence team, angels can take classes through their angel group or at the Angel Capital Association (ACA).

Diversification can be the key to success, or at least the key to minimizing risk in any investing, and this applies to early-stage investing, too. Any investment professional, from your local financial planner to Jim Cramer on CNBC, will tell you to "make sure you have a diversified portfolio." What does that mean, and how do you do that?

We have a saying in angel world, and I'm not sure who came up with it. The saying goes: "Out of ten companies, five will fail, three will return the money invested, one will return the investment with a small return, and one may hit with a larger return." So, how do you decide which of the ten to invest in? The more companies an investor gets exposure to, the lower the risk becomes that all money will be lost. Until recently, angels mainly invested directly into one company at a time. However, investing in an angel fund allows an individual to make one investment, which is spread by the fund across multiple companies, much like a mutual fund works in the public markets. And what about the companies that don't make it? The start-up world is a learning experience. The most successful founders have had failures in their past. I try to think about the companies that don't make it not as failures but more as sources of lessons that will make the next innovation or company more likely to succeed. Think about how many times Thomas Edison tried before he invented the light bulb.

The number one reason start-ups go out of business is because they run out of money. This sometimes happens because of an entrepreneur's inexperience in managing money, or it could be because the company didn't meet the milestones investors anticipated—making it difficult to garner future investor interest.

Start-ups should raise at least twelve, preferably eighteen to twenty-four, months of needed capital when they go out to investors. This is called a round of funding. The stages of rounds are as follows:

- Friends and Family—the earliest money raise
- Series Seed—the first angel or outside money
- Series A—significant milestones have been hit attracting bigger investors
- Series B—a growth round: Venture Capitalists (VCs) will start to become interested
- Any Series from C Onward—usually VCs only

I've made many mistakes investing in early-stage companies. They are all risky, and there is always a reason to say no. But as you look more closely at the founders and innovations and look at many companies over time, you can find your yeses—those start-ups that align with your Halo Strategy and have enough potential to grow in value and impact.

Diversification is not putting all your eggs in the same basket. Some say invest in at least ten companies but thirty or even fifty baskets would be better.

In the last five years, I've seen many more angel funds allowing people to invest as little as $5,000. Before angel funds became more available, venture capital fund minimums averaged $250,000; only the super-wealthy could participate. Funds can make you an investor in ten, fifteen, or even twenty-plus companies by just writing one check—making them an ideal way for new angels to get started.

It's also worth noting that angels may choose to invest in later funding rounds to maintain their percentage of ownership, or pro-rata, in the company. This strategy, known as keeping "dry powder," involves setting aside funds specifically for such opportunities.

As you can see, there is a lot to evaluate and consider in the due diligence phase. This workbook is meant to give you the exercises and activities to find your why, get a basic understanding of how to evaluate a start-up, and figure out how you may get started. We did not cover all of due diligence here. There are many courses and educational materials out there where you can learn more. And don't worry. You don't have to do due diligence on your own. Finding an angel group or fund can help make it far easier to do a full vetting of the company, and getting to know other angels and going through the process can be fun, too.

Part III

GET STARTED

You have found your *why* and *the how* of deciding whether to invest your time and money in an early-stage company. Now let's look at how to get started, which can be easy, simple, and fun.

In this section, we will break down the ways you can:

- Invest with Your Time
- Find an Angel Group
- Get Started with a Small Amount of Time or Money
- Invest Using Philanthropic Dollars, Your IRA, and Through Funds

You will also have the opportunity to create a mock portfolio using play money and an online crowdfunding platform, so you can gain initial hands-on experience with no risk.

If you have a spouse or partner, it will be helpful for them to understand your interest in supporting early-stage companies, so they can be supportive or even get involved.

Thus, we will wrap up this section with activities to facilitate smoother conversations about investment endeavors with family members or friends. (If desired, feel free to review this section first.)

INVEST WITH YOUR TIME

Individuals interested in angel investing can begin by offering their expertise to assist a start-up in need. If you are not ready to invest money and want to learn more about start-ups, investing time and volunteering your expertise is a great way to support start-ups locally. This doesn't require advanced degrees, as valuable contributions can range from bookkeeping to client outreach to reviewing hiring practices—the opportunities to assist an early-stage company are vast.

Entrepreneurs also thrive on encouragement—a bit of cheerleading can make a significant difference. Indeed, launching and expanding a business is challenging, with some days proving tougher than others. Having supportive confidants to discuss and refine ideas with can be incredibly valuable. Without strong support systems, entrepreneurs often drive themselves to the brink of burnout, potentially losing crucial time that could otherwise be spent advancing their business. A supportive voice can provide motivation and a much-needed perspective to help keep their efforts balanced and productive.

Activity: To connect with a start-up, consider attending local start-up or pitch events, or exploring accelerators. Accelerators are business programs that provide mentorship and advice to growing companies. Sometimes accelerators are stand-alone organizations; other times they might be affiliated with community development organizations or universities. These groups are excellent ways to build relationships and apply your time and talent in meaningful ways. Open your favorite search engine and search for "start-up events near me" or "start-up accelerators near me." Document what you find and copy the list of skills, talents, and expertise you made in *The Value You Bring Beyond Dollars* in Part I, so you have it all in one place. Make a plan of what you will do over the next month or so to get started.

Bonus content not in the book *Do Good While Doing Well*: In the fall of 2023, Susie deVille, author of *Buoyant, The Entrepreneur's Guide to Becoming Wildly Successful, Creative, and Free*, was on *The Angel Next Door* podcast. Susie challenges the conventional wisdom often given to entrepreneurs and creators, which typically emphasizes a formulaic approach to achieving success—essentially, working harder, with more discipline, and pushing oneself to the limit with the mindset of "sleeping when you're dead."

She argues against the inefficient method of striving for success, likening it to digging a tunnel with a teaspoon—while it's possible, it's hardly an ideal strategy. This perspective stems from her previous belief that hard work was directly linked to personal worth. This belief is a common trap, reflecting a cultural misconception that equates value with the ability to demonstrate hard work and perseverance.

Susie believes in the intricate relationship among creativity, self-trust, and business success, particularly amidst the uncertainties entrepreneurs face. By nurturing and harnessing creativity, entrepreneurs can unlock new pathways to success that extend far beyond traditional notions of hustle and grind. Entrepreneurs—and the angels who support them—can tap into creative reservoirs by incorporating Susie's five elements of success (what she calls The 5Ms™): morning pages (the brainchild of author Julia Cameron), meditation, movement, moments of inspired learning, and making something into their routine. This not only fosters a sense of alignment with our authentic selves but also opens doors to fresh perspectives and unprecedented solutions in the entrepreneurial journey. When entrepreneurs have genuine enthusiasm and unhampered energy for their venture, it can make all the difference in attracting the right support and ideal client base. By leveraging a harmonious blend of strategic acumen and creative ingenuity, entrepreneurs can elevate their resilience, forge meaningful connections, and ultimately chart a course toward a fulfilling and successful entrepreneurial endeavor.

Entrepreneurs and those who invest in, mentor, and support them—well, everyone for that matter—could all benefit from embracing this philosophy, incorporating creativity into our busy lives of business building, leadership, and life overall.

Activity: Think outside of the business box. Bringing creativity and this notion of helping an entrepreneur by having them take a step outside of the day-to-day can be very valuable. This might involve something as simple as a shared stroll through a park or city, offering exposure to new environments. Alternatively, consider spending an afternoon together exploring a museum or taking an art class. Compile a list of creative activities you enjoy and explore how they could support an entrepreneur. Many of these activities are probably either free or low-cost. You can easily find free events in your area by searching online. Who knows, you might stumble upon something new and exciting to explore together.

FIND AN ANGEL GROUP

The traditional, and until 2020, predominant method of angel investing was through "angel groups." These groups, often local or regional, sometimes have specific industry focuses, and geographic boundaries don't necessarily dictate membership. The COVID pandemic forced so many angel activities to move online, which broadened their reach. Before the pandemic, becoming a member of an angel group, like Queen City Angels (QCA) in Cincinnati, Ohio, was uncommon if you didn't live in the area. Now, QCA and many angel groups take members from all over the country and hold most meetings in a hybrid style, if not completely online. This means you can join an angel group no matter where you live.

Doing a simple online search for "angel groups near me" can help you see if there is an angel group in your local community. From there, you may find their website or a way to contact the organizer of the group to get information about upcoming meetings and the type of companies the group invests in. There are some large, well-known, national angel groups in the US that allow investors from any part of the country to become members. You can also visit angelcapitalassociation.org to find a list of angel groups.

> *Activity:* Go to your favorite search engine and look up "angel groups in _____" and fill in where you live. Or you could look for "angel groups investing in _____" and fill in something like "life sciences" or "healthcare" or maybe "women-led companies," depending on what you identified as your top three causes during Part I.

DIVERSIFY WITH FUNDS

As a traditional angel, investing directly into a company or even through an angel group requires thousands of dollars; the average could be $5,000 to $25,000 in a single company. In ACA's education classes, it is taught that a diversified portfolio needs to have at least ten companies in it. My personal experience has shown thirty is a better number. So, imagine having to write thirty $25,000 checks to try to get a truly diversified portfolio. Only a fraction of a percentage of the US population could even consider that. The best way I have found to get a diversified portfolio is by investing in funds. Venture capital funds requiring a lower minimum to invest (say $10,000 or $25,000 instead of $250,000) are becoming more prevalent. I call these *angel funds* since they are typically angels who are investing. Finding an angel fund to invest in may take some research or networking because the SEC regulations around funds do not allow for them to "solicit" investors publicly. To find a fund to consider investing in, ask at the local start-up event you might be attending from the activity in this workbook's "Invest with Your Time" section. Many angel groups have funds.

GET STARTED WITH A SMALL AMOUNT OF MONEY AND A LITTLE BIT OF TIME

Regulation Crowdfunding (Reg CF) was created as part of the 2012 JOBS act (see glossary for details), but the rules around implementation weren't finalized until 2016. Reg CF is a regulatory framework that allows non-accredited investors to invest in privately held small businesses as long as they go through a regulated funding portal or platform. Businesses seeking to raise capital, also known as issuers by the SEC, must follow specific rules. Below are three ways to invest with as little as $50 to $100 using a bank account or credit card and an internet connection, making it relatively easy for someone, regardless of wealth or income, to invest.

- Equity Crowdfunding (EC)
- Debt Crowdfunding (DC)
- Revenue-based Financing Crowdfunding (RBF)

Equity and debt crowdfunding enables individuals to invest a modest amount of money in a company, offering different returns. With EC, investors receive a proportional ownership stake in the company, while DC involves repayment over time, similar to a traditional loan with regular payment schedules. RBF also allows individuals to invest a small sum, but investors are repaid based on the company's revenue performance.

Crowdfunding has evolved significantly over the last several years, transitioning from donation and reward models to include equity stakes, debt financing, and revenue share for small businesses.

Equity crowdfunding (EC) enables investors to pool their resources with others to acquire an ownership stake in a business. Investments in private companies often require patience, as they may take time to reach a liquidity event where investors can cash out. Therefore, start-ups with significant growth potential tend to be more appealing for this type of investing.

Debt (DC) and revenue-based financing (RBF) crowdfunding typically offer quicker liquidity, with regular payments made over time. These opportunities often involve "main street" businesses rather than scalable start-ups. These are stable, small businesses usually located in your neighborhood or town, providing essential services to the community.

DEBT CROWDFUNDING — BONUS CONTENT NOT IN THE BOOK, DO GOOD WHILE DOING WELL

Debt crowdfunding (DC), as exemplified by platforms like Honeycomb Credit, whose CEO George Cook appeared on *The Angel Next Door* podcast in April 2024, represents a pragmatic choice for many small businesses that traditionally struggle with rigid banking conditions or may not foresee a big liquidity event or a way to sell the company so investors can eventually get a return.

Main street businesses like the local coffee shop or dry cleaners could benefit from this type of funding. These stable, well-performing businesses need capital to grow but are sometimes overlooked by traditional financing channels. Through debt crowdfunding platforms, businesses apply and go through a vetting process that involves financial history checks, owners' credit checks, and background checks. Once approved, they can be on the platform to present their business and plans to potential investors. Debt agreements can range from three to five years, offering a fixed return without giving up equity in the business.

Investors are often the business's customers and community members. They can invest through an online system with ease in a process that emphasizes the personal and local nature of the investment. Some businesses will even put a QR code on a sign at checkout to promote the campaign.

The repayment process is designed for clarity and regularity, with businesses making monthly payments back to the platform in order to make distributions to investors on a quarterly basis. The appeal to investors is multifaceted—there is the financial return on investment, coupled with the satisfaction of contributing to the growth of businesses they frequent or believe in. Honeycomb Credit and platforms like it are not only democratizing investment opportunities for non-traditional investors but are also providing a vital source of funding for an underserved segment of the business community, fostering growth and innovation. Chapter Two of *Do Good While Doing Well* has more information about crowdfunding.

Revenue-based financing (RBF) crowdfunding allows someone to loan capital in exchange for a percentage of ongoing gross revenues but not own any part of the company. With revenue-based financing, you could invest a small amount of money, like $100, in exchange for a portion of the coffee shop's future revenues. Instead of receiving a percentage of ownership which could take a long time to translate into a return (as we saw with EC), you'll start receiving regular payments based on the coffee shop's sales. It's a win-win situation because your investment grows as the business thrives, and you get to be a part of the coffee shop's success story.

While similar, the main difference between debt (DC) and revenue-based financing (RBF) crowdfunding lies in the repayment structure. In debt crowdfunding, investors provide a loan to the company, which is repaid over time with interest, typically following a fixed schedule. On the other hand, revenue-based financing involves investors receiving a percentage of the company's future revenues until an agreed-upon amount is repaid (such as 1.5 times multiple), without requiring fixed payments or interest.

To find an online platform to get started, search for what you are looking for such as "equity crowdfunding platforms." Once there, you can browse the companies that are currently fundraising and see what interests you. Just browse first and read through the information. Be sure to read the comment section; that is where the CEO or founders put the answers to all the questions. When raising money on one of these sites, the management team is not allowed to answer questions off the site, like in email. Every question and answer must be documented on the platform, so everyone has the same information in order to make an investment decision.

Regulation Crowdfunding has only been around since 2016, and it's still in its very early days. We still need to see plenty of innovation for:

- The Platforms—if you google "best equity or debt crowdfunding sites," the results will give you plenty of places to check out. Many, though, assume you know what crowdfunding is before you get there, making the user experience cumbersome.

- The number of start-ups using equity or debt crowdfunding—while there is an increasing number of start-ups raising capital this way, the number of choices of where to invest is still relatively limited.

- Searching for the change you want to see in the world—many of the sites don't allow for searching by cause or category. You can search by industry or company size, but if you try to search with something like "cure cancer," you probably won't find what you are looking for, even if there are start-ups on the platform whose businesses fit that criteria.

No matter how you start searching, you are bound to find something that aligns with your goal of making change in the world. Of course, don't forget the golden rule in early-stage investing—look for a while before making an actual investment. You will learn a lot by just browsing. I wish equity, debt, and RBF crowdfunding had been around when I started angel investing. The transparency required of the start-ups on these platforms is very educational and can help get you started on this interesting and rewarding journey.

The beauty of equity and debt crowdfunding generally, and this type of RBF specifically, is that it levels the playing field for investors of all backgrounds. Whether you're a student, a working professional, or a retiree, you can now support local businesses and potential unicorns without breaking the bank. It's a grassroots movement that empowers individuals to invest in the businesses they believe in, making dreams come true one small investment at a time.

Likely, by the time you are reading this, even more creative opportunities will have come to light. In addition, some of the platforms referenced in this workbook may be gone, and new ones may have emerged. To see an updated list, go to **www.marciadawood.com/dogood**.

CREATE A MOCK PORTFOLIO

Now that you know the basics about these three types of crowdfunding, let's have some fun with fake dollars. Imagine you have $2,500 of play money and find at least ten companies you would like to invest in. You may also want to include a family member(s), friend or two as you complete this activity. The conversation around the dinner table could get quite interesting.

> *Activity:* Create a Mock Portfolio—The objective of this exercise is to familiarize yourself with equity, debt and/or RBF crowdfunding platforms and develop a better understanding of the investment process.
>
> Instructions:
>
> 1. Choose a Crowdfunding Platform: Select an equity, debt, or RBF crowdfunding platform. I suggest a more well-known one, such as Honeycomb Credit, Republic, StartEngine or Wefunder. I used Republic.com.
>
> 2. Explore Investment Opportunities: Browse the featured investment opportunities or campaigns on the platform's homepage or by searching.
>
> 3. Search for Companies: Use the platform's search or browse function to find companies that align with your investment interests or criteria. Use

keywords related to industries, technologies, or business models. (Keep in mind that the functionality of these platforms is improving, but you could still encounter some limitations.)

4. Evaluate Company Profiles: Click on several company profiles to learn more about their business, team, and investment opportunity. Review the problem they are solving, the market potential, growth strategies—all you learned about in Part II of this workbook. Use your Halo Navigator™ list of questions.

5. Do a Halo Navigator™ Deeper Dive: Once you find a company that interests you and you have screened them with your list of initial questions, look for materials provided by the companies to help fill out your Halo Navigator™ Deeper Dive worksheet on the next page. Review the communication section on the selected platform to see comments and other questions that have been asked and answered by the CEO or team.

In Part II of this workbook (under the heading "After the Pitch"), there was a list of questions related to doing a deeper dive. The same questions are presented in the Halo Navigator Deeper Dive worksheet. This worksheet will help you go deeper with your assessment of potential angel investments. While the questions are similar to those on the Halo Navigator worksheet used for screening, this worksheet encourages a deeper examination of various aspects. You may want to conduct further online research or review additional materials on the platform to gather more information. Additionally, you might want to discuss your thoughts or questions with a friend or partner for additional perspective. Don't hesitate to ask questions to the CEO or team members on the platform as well.

There is one copy immediately below, and three more copies at the end of this workbook, to get you started: write directly on the worksheets in this workbook, or rip one out and make more copies.

Keep in mind that a full due diligence review will be done by a group of angels or a fund. Due diligence courses also exist to help people learn more of the details. You can find out more at angelcapitalassociation.org under education.

Halo Navigator™ Deeper Dive

The team - Who do they have and need to make this a success?
_____
_____
_____

The addressable market - Who wants what they are selling?
_____
_____
_____

The competition - Who else is doing this?
_____
_____
_____

The product - Does it work? Will people use it?
_____
_____
_____

The business model - Do or will they make money? Is this a company that can be sold down the road and investors will make money?
_____
_____
_____

The offering - How much money are they asking for, and what specifically do they plan to do with it?
_____
_____
_____

The term sheet (if they have one yet): What details can investors expect to get for their money?
_____
_____

6. Select Investments for your Mock Portfolio: Imagine you have $2,500 and use this play money to create a mock investment portfolio consisting of at least ten companies from your selected crowdfunding platform. Based on your Halo Strategy™ answers so far, allocate a total of $2,500 of play money across these companies. You don't need to spread the dollars equally. If you like one company more than another or the investment minimums require it, you can allocate to each company differently.

7. Tracking: The Investment Tracker on the next page will give you a place to keep a record of all the mock investments in your mock portfolio. If you were to actually invest, you could also monitor the performance of your mock portfolio over time by keeping track of any updates, news, or developments related to each company as you would typically get updates from the crowdfunding site.

    Congratulations! You've taken an important first step toward investing for change.

    You've completed the exercise on exploring crowdfunding platforms and creating a mock investment portfolio. By researching investment opportunities and simulating investment decisions, you've gained practical experience in evaluating potential investments and managing a diversified portfolio. Take a few minutes to compare the mission of each company in your mock portfolio and the list you made in Part I related to the changes you want to see in the world. Do they match? When reviewing actual companies, what drew your interest the most?

Investment Tracker

Company Name	Date of Investment	Amount Invested	Why you invested	Change the company is working on for the world	Date the Campaign ends/ended	Valuation or cap (if applicable)	Notes

INVEST WITH PHILANTHROPIC DOLLARS

"Wait—I can donate to charity and invest at the same time? How does that work?" This was my reaction when I first learned about investing through a donor-advised fund (DAF). A DAF is a personal charitable account set up to hold money or securities to donate to 501(c)(3) organizations. According to Fidelity Charitable, DAFs are the fastest-growing charitable vehicle in the US due to their ease of use and their many tax advantages. For example, let's say you received a bonus from your employer and want to donate a portion of it to charity. You're not sure you will get a bonus next year, and you want to continue your giving plan. Rather than give the entire amount this year, you could open a DAF and set up grants to go to charity (or charities) over several years. The entire amount committed to the DAF is tax deductible in the current year, and while the funds are sitting in the DAF, they can grow tax free. The one caveat is the assets within the DAF can never go back to the donor.

Many people have the money within their DAF invested in stocks, bonds, or mutual funds so the funds will grow until the grants are made to the charitable organizations. However, a little-known secret is that in a self-directed DAF, the money can be invested in private companies or start-ups as well. The returns go back into the self-directed DAF, which can then be either reinvested in another start-up or donated to a charity. This enables the donor to amplify their impact by investing in areas like healthcare or supporting underrepresented founders and potentially benefiting from significant financial returns if the start-up succeeds. This approach is also attractive for those who cannot directly invest in a start-up because investing from a DAF does not require the investor to meet the accredited investor requirements.

Custodians who manage and oversee assets that specifically handle self-directed DAFs are listed on my website at **www.marciadawood.com/dogood**.

An example of DAF dollars in action is Daintree Capital, an investment firm providing working capital loans to underrepresented entrepreneurs founded by Alisha Griffey. Instead of the traditional fund-raising route, Alisha chose to leverage donor-advised funds (DAFs) to creatively harness charitable capital for investing in for-profit businesses. Daintree targets companies with revenue between $100,000 and $2 million, offering loans ranging from $10,000 to $75,000 to boost inventory and drive near-term revenue.

Bonus content not in the book *Do Good While Doing Well*: In March of 2024, I met Patrice and Leah Brickman, a mother/daughter dynamic duo who co-founded Inspire Access, a visionary 501(c)(3) organization dedicated to revolutionizing philanthropic capital investment to support underrepresented founders. During a compelling interview on *The Angel Next Door* podcast, they shared their journey toward addressing the issue of women and people of color receiving a disproportionately small share of investment capital—a theme I've explored throughout *Do Good While Doing Well*. With their extensive background in business and philanthropy, they saw the untapped potential of leveraging charity donations to significantly alter the flow of investment capital toward those who traditionally lack access. This could both help underrepresented start-up founders and potentially grow those philanthropic dollars to help more charitable organizations in the future.

So how did they do this?

They understood the amount of money sitting in donor-advised funds (DAFs) amounted to hundreds of billions of dollars—most of which could be self-directed to invest in start-ups. They also realized that Inspire Access could funnel philanthropic capital toward underrepresented founders building for-profit companies using money from DAFs and by making direct donations since Inspire Access operates as a 501(c)(3) themselves. This model fuels impactful ventures and provides donors with tax advantages and the possibility of recycling financial returns into further philanthropic efforts. Inspire Access does not hold capital waiting to find worthy entrepreneurs (as there are many), rather, they encourage all donors to direct their donations by choosing a start-up as soon as the donation is made to get funding to the companies faster.

At its core, Inspire Access prioritizes the entrepreneur over the industry, focusing its resources on ensuring that underrepresented founders have the necessary capital to navigate early-stage challenges. This approach has allowed them to support various companies through direct equity investments and be able to invest in venture capital funds, supporting many first-time fund managers without being bound by sector-specific constraints.

Throughout our conversation, Patrice and Leah shared success stories, demonstrating the profound difference even minimal investments can make in the trajectories of these underprivileged entrepreneurs, especially in the very early days.

The insights from Patrice and Leah complement my message of *Do Good While Doing Well* and serve as a practical example of how innovative thinking in philanthropy and investment can address systemic inequalities. Their work with Inspire Access is a testament to the power of combining financial resources with a commitment to social equity, offering a tangible model for effecting positive change.

INVEST FROM YOUR IRA

Many people choose to save for retirement with individual retirement accounts (IRAs) because of the tax advantages. In a traditional IRA, you get your tax benefits upfront—a kind of immediate gratification. Your money grows in this sheltered environment, free from tax until you withdraw it. Roth IRAs play the long game. You pay your taxes upfront, and your investments grow tax-free. Either way, it's like planting a seed in fertile soil and watching it flourish.

Your IRA doesn't have to be just a retirement vessel. It can be a vehicle for change, a tool for transforming start-ups into game-changing enterprises. The story of Peter Thiel turning his PayPal shares into billions via a Roth IRA is more than a financial legend; it's a testament to the untapped potential sitting in retirement accounts nationwide. Thiel took early shares of PayPal when they were worth a small amount of money and put them into a Roth IRA. A Roth IRA allows investments to grow tax free because taxes are paid upfront when the dollars or stock is put into the account. In Thiel's case, his shares of PayPal grew to more than $5 billion. You can read more about this in a Forbes article from June 2021, also available on my website's book resources page.

While investing in start-ups does have its risks and caveats, using funds from an IRA offers a compelling alternative if you are seeking impactful investments without immediate liquidity. This is done through a self-directed individual retirement account (SDIRA).

IRAs are usually considered financial instruments that contain bonds, stocks, and mutual funds. The SDIRAs can have all those things and more. While most people associate IRAs with retirement savings—and rightly so—an SDIRA presents an exciting pathway for those passionate about investing in start-ups. This isn't just a traditional IRA with a twist; it's a flexible vehicle that allows you to channel funds into nontraditional investments, including private companies in their infancy. Think of it as a win-win: You get to diversify your portfolio while potentially significantly impacting the next generation of innovative companies.

The big brokerage houses usually don't allow self-directed activity. Understanding the mechanics of investing through a SDIRA is essential for both start-ups and individual investors. The process involves two steps, which both parties must complete to ensure a successful investment.

The first step for start-ups looking to raise funds is to submit all necessary company information to the SDIRA custodian. This specialized entity manages these types of investment accounts. Consider this as the due diligence phase, where the entrepreneur presents their company's credentials to become a qualified investment option. This isn't a mere rubber stamp. It's a crucial fiduciary exercise where the custodian reviews the start-up's financial credentials, ensuring they meet all legal standards. The company is approved and included on the custodian's investment platform.

As an investor, your first step is to open and fund your SDIRA account. Your next step is to inform the custodian about your investment preferences, specifying that you wish to invest in a particular start-up that has already been set up on their platform. Both parties must be in sync.

The invest-for-change potential with SDIRAs is quite large. In 1995, IRAs housed about $1.3 trillion. Fast-forward to today, and that amount has ballooned to nearly $10 trillion. That is a vast ocean of untapped resources, some of which could be channeled into groundbreaking early-stage companies.

In 2019, I assisted a start-up in navigating these waters. With a couple of straightforward forms, we successfully listed their offering on Mainstar Trust's SDIRA platform. From there, investors, me included, were able to use funds from our SDIRA accounts to propel this start-up forward. It was easier than I thought it would be since I didn't fund my new SDIRA with cash. I took an existing IRA account from Fidelity and moved it to Mainstar. My investment into the start-up was made from there. And I was also able to invest in public stocks as well.

Important note: If and when the start-up succeeds, and you cash out, that money goes right back into your IRA. If you've reached the fifty-nine-and-a-half-year-old age, you can take distributions without penalty and enjoy the fruits of your investment right away. If not, the funds must stay in the IRA until you are eligible for distributions. In the meantime, you could invest in another start-up or fund or put the gains into another asset of your choice.

But hold on; there's an asterisk here. When you turn seventy-three, you must take "mandatory" distributions from your IRA. However, liquidity can become a stumbling block. What if the start-up you invested in hasn't gone public or been acquired? Your investment is still tied up, complicating your distribution requirements. The remedy can be simple: diversification. Have enough liquid assets in your IRA to maneuver around these bumps in the road. For mandatory distributions, you can also move a portion of your stock from your SDIRA to another account, solving the liquidity conundrum.

The next time you think about early-stage investments, consider the role a self-directed IRA could play. With more and more SDIRA custodians appearing, this pathway is increasingly accessible for those who want to make change in the world. Go to **www.marciadawood.com/dogood** for a list of SDIRA custodians.

TAX ADVANTAGES FOR ANGELS

Even some of the most experienced angels don't know about tax advantages that both entrepreneurs and angels have under what is called the qualified small business stock (QSBS) gain exclusion. People may refer to this as QSBS, or 1202 for short. Section 1202 of the IRS tax code exempts shareholders from paying capital gains taxes on QSBS stock they have held for more than five years. "Shareholders" in this case could include founders, management teams, advisors, board members, investors—anyone who owns stock. This is a big deal.

QSBS was set up to promote long-term investment. One of the other benefits not regularly discussed is that an investor who sees a gain from owning stock in a private company is encouraged to use the gain to invest in another private company—so that the cycle of promoting innovation continues. In 2020, my first angel investment from 2012 was bought by another company, yielding me a 3x return on my investment. Because I held that stock for over five years, I did not have to pay any capital gains tax on the profit. Keep in mind that I did use after-tax dollars to make the investment.

To learn more about this, check out two *The Angel Next Door* podcast episodes—one with Tony Shipley and one with Jeff Soloman. Of course, you can also go to the book resources page on my website to find out the latest information on tax advantages for angels.

TIME FOR ACTION

Now that you have completed several activities to figure out what resonates with you related to investing for change, let's complete the Halo Strategy™ worksheet and formulate an action plan.

Activity: Let's Discover How You Want to Contribute.

Determine how best you can support the causes close to your heart—through time, talent, or treasure. Over the years, I have done a mix of all three. Sometimes, I find I don't have any extra money to support my cause. During those times, I tend to give more time and talent.

Time: Ask yourself, How many hours can I realistically dedicate monthly?

Talent: In Chapter 1, you made a list of your skills, talent, and expertise. Ask yourself, How can my specific talents benefit my chosen causes?

Treasure: Consider your financial capacity. Even small contributions can have big impacts. Ask yourself, How much money would I be willing to invest to help the causes I care about? Over what time period? Monthly? Annually?

Make-a-Contribution Plan. For example, "I will work with entrepreneurs three hours a month (time), offer one bookkeeping review (talent), and invest $1,000 annually (treasure)."

Remember, every little bit counts. Plus, the way you choose to contribute is personal to you and your capabilities, which vary at different times of the year and stages of life.

Write your answer(s) in the "How I want to contribute" box on your Halo Strategy™ worksheet.

Activity: Think about what makes sense for your timing. You could start by searching online if there is a local angel group in your area or any upcoming start-up events or exploring a crowdfunding website.

Make a commitment that you will do something to start your angel investment journey in the next week, two weeks, or a month at the latest. The journey can start right away with exploration and by simply learning more about entrepreneurial activity going on near you.

Write your answer(s) in the "When I Will Start" box on your Halo Strategy™ worksheet.

Activity: Think about what makes sense with how much time or money you would like to invest. This could be over a period of time, such as I will invest five hours a month for the next year, and I will set aside $xx over the next year to make at least five investments or invest in at least one fund. Remember, many angels limit their investments in early-stage companies to just 5 to 10 percent of their investable assets and set a maximum dollar amount for these investments.

Write your answer(s) in the "How much time/money I will start with?" box on your Halo Strategy™ worksheet.

MAKING INVESTMENT DECISIONS WITH A PARTNER/SPOUSE OR FAMILY

When Izzy and I made our first angel investment, we discussed questions about the company itself, but I don't remember talking very much about how each of us *felt* about making the investment. Did it fit with the changes we wanted to see in the world? Did it align with our overall long-term financial goals? Considering that all investments come with risk, how would each of us feel if we lost all the money? Sometimes, talking about money can be tough, especially getting the conversation started. In this section, let's explore any apprehension you may have in talking to your spouse/partner or family about money, short-term and long-term goals, and investing for change. We will explore ways to get conversations started and give some prompts to help guide the discussions along the way.

Activity: Reflect on past conversations about important topics with significant individuals in your life. Maybe the issues included where you live or work. Maybe goals for the future such as buying a home, supporting children's education or aging family members, or planning for your retirement. Write or draw about how you felt. Did you think the discussions were productive? What could have been different?

Activity: Write or draw your thoughts on the following questions:

What are your financial goals and priorities?

Are there any specific money-related anxieties or concerns you have?

Activity: Schedule a time to sit down with your partner/family and discuss your shared financial goals. If it is helpful, use the space provided to write out what you want to say ahead of time to set up this meeting. You may want to mention your desire to discuss the family's short- and long-term goals and a vision for your financial future.

Preparing for the conversation—when it comes to how to think and feel about money related to angel investing, investing $50 or $250 is one thing, but how about investing $20,000 or $250,000 as you build your portfolio? Now the stakes have changed, and the conversations need to be much different. This is the main reason I encourage all new angels to take the time to "just watch." Like people browse for cars or houses, be an observer and see many different companies before even considering an investment. And not just a quick glance; review the pitch materials and participate in some due diligence on ten or even twenty companies before investing. This will take time, and that's OK. Maybe even up to six months or a year, and that's also OK. Start-ups work at lightning speed, and they will tell you they have some incredibly tight deadlines, but there will always be start-ups to invest in, so don't get overwhelmed. It is better to observe and learn and invest wisely (or as wisely as you can) than to rush and regret.

Taking this time can help make the discussion with your partner much easier and fun, too. More and more, I've had couples tell me how much their evening dinner conversations have changed since learning about angel investing, and how they are talking about things they have never talked about before. Discussing the life-changing innovations that start-ups are creating can be fun and exciting.

Activity: Now that you set a time with your partner/family, use the Halo Communicator™ worksheet as a guide to start the discussion. You may want to take some time before the meeting for each of you to fill out the worksheet on your own and then compare your answers. Or you can fill it out together. Whatever you feel more comfortable doing. Remember that money can be a sensitive subject, so listen carefully and be kind as you have these conversations.

Halo Communicator™ Worksheet

Here are some discussion prompts for couples or families related to money, to ensure alignment and clarity before making any investment decisions

Financial Goals:

What are your short-term and long-term financial goals? Do you have a strategy to achieve your goals?

_____
_____
_____
_____

Communication:

How do you communicate now related to investment decisions? How will you communicate with each other about investment decisions in the future?

_____
_____
_____
_____

Risk Tolerance:

How comfortable are you with the risks associated with investing of any kind? How do you feel about risks vs rewards? Are you both/all on the same page regarding your risk tolerance? How would you feel if you lost money on an investment?

_____
_____
_____
_____

Impact:

How important is it for you to invest in opportunities that align with your values or have a positive social impact? How important is it for you to consider the potential social or environmental impact of your investments?

_____
_____
_____
_____

Investment Amount:

How much of your money is invested? Where are the investments? Public markets? Real Estate? Private markets?

_____
_____
_____
_____

Financial Goals:

What are your short-term and long-term financial goals? Do you have a strategy to achieve your goals?

_____
_____
_____
_____

Time Horizon:

What is your investment time horizon? Are you willing to hold an investment for the long term, understanding that returns may
take years to materialize?

_____
_____
_____
_____

FINAL STEPS

Regardless of where you are on your journey to do good while doing well, there are a vast number of ways to participate, and there are new developments in this area every day.

Now, you are at the point of developing an action plan. This is the last section of your Halo Strategy™ worksheet. You have several ideas from throughout this workbook. Whatever you decide, just get started. It is the best way to learn and make a difference at the same time.

Activity: Review all the sections of Part III of this workbook to see what way of getting started resonates with you the most. Maybe there are a few different ways. Use the space provided to write or draw your ideas of your action plan and then add the first three steps you will take to the three action plan boxes at the bottom of your Halo Strategy™ worksheet.

As you complete the *Do Good While Doing Well* workbook, it should be evident that you've embarked on a transformative journey toward becoming an impactful investor with a clear sense of purpose and direction. By identifying your why for wanting to see change and understanding what you care about deeply, you've laid a solid foundation for your investment journey. Armed with the knowledge and skills to evaluate deals effectively, you're more equipped to make informed investment decisions that align with your values and aspirations.

As you step into the world of angel investing, remember that your journey is just beginning. Each investment opportunity presents a chance to make a difference and contribute to positive change in the world. Stay true to your why, remain open to learning and growth, and continue to leverage your resources and influence for the greater good. By combining financial returns with social and societal impact, you have the power to shape a more equitable and sustainable future for generations to come. Embrace the journey with confidence and conviction, knowing that your efforts have the potential to create ripples of change that will echo worldwide.

A FAVOR

I could use your help! If you found this book valuable, please take a minute or two to share your thoughts in a review. Reviews are so meaningful to the success of the book, its reach and impact. I would greatly appreciate it. You can leave a review on Amazon or Goodreads by searching for *Do Good While Doing Well*.

LET'S START A CONVERSATION

Reach out to ask questions or discuss ways I can help you.

www.marciadawood.com

@marciadawood on IG

marciadawood on LinkedIn

Please visit **www.marciadawood.com/dogood** to download extra worksheet pages.

GLOSSARY

Several of these terms were not used in this book, but I've included them in case you need them as you venture into angel world.

- **ACA—Angel Capital Association**: The professional association of angel investors in the US offering education, membership benefits, networking, and public policy advocacy.

- **Accredited Investor**: A definition set in place by the US Securities and Exchange Commission. As of 2023, it is based mainly on income and wealth levels. The investor must make an annual income of $200,000 if single ($300,000 with a spouse) or have $1 million in net worth, excluding the primary home.

- **Angel Group**: A formal or informal organization of individuals who come together to evaluate start-up investment opportunities in order to make angel investments.

- **Angel Investor**: An individual who provides support (money, time, or expertise) to start-ups or entrepreneurs, often in exchange for convertible debt or ownership equity.

- **AOV**: Average Order Value. The metric that tracks the average dollar amount spent on each order.

- **ARR**: Annual Recurring Revenue. The amount of normalized annual revenue from existing subscriptions.

- **B2B (Business-to-Business)**: Refers to businesses primarily selling products or services to other businesses rather than directly to consumers.

- **Bootstrapping**: Building a company from the ground up with nothing but personal savings and the cash coming in from the first sales.

- **Burn Rate**: The rate at which a company is spending its capital before generating positive cash flow from operations.

- **Business Angel**: A term used primarily in Europe for an angel investor.

- **CAC**: Customer Acquisition Cost. The amount of money spent to acquire a new customer.

- **Cap Table**: Stands for capitalization table, which is simply a list of all the investors and the percentage of the company each owns.

- **Capital Gains Tax**: Capital gains are the profit from selling an asset, like a public stock, mutual fund, or private stock. This is different from ordinary income tax, which is the tax you pay on income.

- **CM**: Contribution Margin. A financial measure of sales minus variable costs.

- **Convertible Note**: A short-term debt that converts into equity, usually in conjunction with a future financing round.

- **COGS**: Cost of Goods Sold. The direct cost of making a product or service.

- **Deal Flow**: The rate, volume, and quality of investment opportunities being evaluated at any given time.

- **Donor Advised Fund (DAF)**: A personal charitable account set up to hold money or securities to donate to 501(c)3 organizations.

- **DTC (Direct-to-Consumer)**: Describes companies that sell products or services directly to consumers, bypassing traditional retail channels.

- **Due Diligence**: The comprehensive assessment of a business, typically conducted by investors before making a funding decision.

- **Elevator Pitch**: A brief, persuasive speech used to spark interest in what a start-up is doing.

- **Equity Financing**: The act of raising capital by selling shares of a company—also called a priced round.

- **Exit (Business Exit)**: The strategy or event through which an investor realizes a return on their investment, such as an acquisition or an IPO.

- **Exit Strategy**: A planned approach to liquidating an investor's stake in a company.

- **Freedom to Operate**: This term refers to the ability of a company to develop, manufacture, and sell a product or service without infringing on the intellectual property rights of others. It typically involves conducting a thorough analysis of existing patents and other IP rights to ensure that a new product or technology doesn't violate any existing protections. This is especially important for start-ups in technology and scientific sectors.

- **Friends and Family Round**: The very first money raised by a new company.

- **General Partner (GP)**: The manager of an angel or venture capital fund who makes investment decisions.

- **Initial Public Offering (IPO)**: The process of offering shares of a private corporation to the public in a new stock issuance.

- **JOBS (Jumpstart Our Business Startups) Act of 2012**: President Obama signed this act into law with the primary goal to foster economic growth by making it easier for start-ups and small businesses to raise capital.

- **Lead Investor**: The first, and typically largest, investor in a funding round.

- **Limited Partner (LP)**: An investor in an angel or venture capital fund who has no decision-making rights.

- **Liquidity Event**: An occurrence that allows initial investors in a company to cash out some or all their equity.

- **Major Investor**: An investor putting a certain amount of money into a company, which entitles them to specific information.

- **Non-Dilutive Funding**: Financing that does not require a company to give up equity.

- **OPEX**: Operational Expenditures. The money a company spends to run day-to-day operations.

- **Pitch or Pitch Deck**: Another term for an entrepreneur's presentation of the investment opportunity.

- **Post-money Valuation**: The estimated value of a company after outside financing and/or capital injections are added.

- **Pre-money Valuation**: The valuation of a company prior to an investment or funding.

- **Pro-Rata Rights**: The right of an investor to participate in future funding rounds to maintain their percentage ownership.

- **Revenue-Based Financing**: A method for companies to raise capital in exchange for a percentage of their future revenue.

- **Simple Agreement for Future Equity (SAFE)**: An agreement to receive equity in a future financing round without setting a specific price per share at the time of the initial investment.

- **Seed Funding**: An initial investment to start a business, covering the initial operating expenses of a new venture.

- **Sidecar Fund**: An investment vehicle used alongside a primary investment fund, allowing investors to participate in specific opportunities.

- **Special-Purpose Vehicle (SPV)**: A group of investors who come together to invest in a single project or company, pooling their resources and expertise.

- **Total Addressable Market (TAM)**: The total size of the opportunity for a product or solution.

- **Term Sheet**: A nonbinding agreement outlining the basic terms and conditions under which an investment will be made.

- **Unicorn**: The name used for a start-up company that is valued at over $1 billion.

- **Valuation**: The process of determining a company's or asset's present worth.

- **Venture Capitalist (VC)**: VCs use other people's money to invest, while angels typically use their own after-tax dollars. For a quick two-minute fun, yet educational video about the difference, visit my website to see my Rap Battle: Angel Investor vs. Venture Capitalist at **marciadawood.com.**

- **Vesting**: The process through which an employee or investor earns the right to receive full ownership of certain assets or stock options over time. In the context of start-ups and angel investing, vesting often applies to the equity or stock options granted to founders, employees, and sometimes investors. The purpose of a vesting schedule is to incentivize longevity and commitment; it ensures that these stakeholders remain engaged and contribute to the company's growth over a period before they can claim full ownership of their equity portion. Typically, this involves a "cliff" period (often one year) before any shares are vested, followed by a gradual vesting period (commonly four years), during which the individual earns the right to their full shares.

AUTHOR'S NOTE

Throughout this workbook, I have tried to explain my views on how we can take an active part in getting the innovation and solutions in the world that we really want to see. The things that will make a big difference in our futures but, more importantly, in the futures of our children and beyond. Frankly, I got tired of seeing energetic companies working on life-changing solutions not go anywhere because there simply wasn't enough financial support and human expertise surrounding them.

All content in this workbook is informational and not intended to serve as legal, tax, accounting, or investing advice. At the time of this writing, I serve on the SEC Small Business Capital Formation Advisory Committee; however, my views are my own and not the views of the SEC or my fellow committee colleagues.

Readers should consult their own tax, investing, legal, or accounting advisors before making important financial decisions. All warranties are disclaimed, including accuracy, completeness, and suitability for specific purposes.

I've done my best to show you my journey and many of the mistakes I've made. My hope is that you will act now. If everyone invested just a little bit of time, money, or expertise, imagine the change we would see in the world—a change that could even save the life of someone you love.

ACKNOWLEDGMENTS

My Acknowledgments for this workbook are similar yet slightly different from those for the book *Do Good While Doing Well*. I would not have been able to write either the book or this workbook without having spent many years learning about angel investing and entrepreneurship, and I could not have done that without the encouragement and support of my husband, Izzy.

In 2011, Izzy and I *almost* moved to London. I was working full-time in a corporate career, and suddenly, I was dreaming of a new life in another country. We didn't end up in London, but my dream of a different life continued. Around the time I was invited to my first angel investing meeting and I decided to get an MBA at UNC Chapel Hill. I would have never been able to pursue what I really wanted if Izzy hadn't been not only supportive but also my biggest cheerleader. He helped me see potential in myself and in what I was doing even before I could. For his support and love, I am forever grateful.

My parents were, of course, my first cheerleaders. They always told me I could do and be anything I put my mind to. I wish my mom were still with us; I would love to share this book with her. If you aren't familiar with that story, watch my TEDx talk. A few years after her death, my dad remarried, and I'm grateful he found happiness again, proving no matter how bad things get, there can be light. I know my mom is looking down on us and smiling.

I wouldn't know as much as I do today if I hadn't had such a great role model in Catherine Mott. Thank you for not just guiding me, but for all the people you have influenced to help make change in the world.

Through angel investing, I was lucky enough to meet people who have become good friends, especially my Next Wave crew. Special thank you to Sue Bevan Baggott who helped tremendously with my TEDx speech, the book as well as this workbook. Sue also introduced me to the Recognized Expert Group (REx) led by Dorie Clark, and Heroic Public Speaking, led by Michael and Amy Port. At Heroic, I learned how to write and deliver a speech, and it is also where I met AJ Harper. Big thanks to AJ and Laura Stone for the wisdom, guidance, and encouragement—and for building the amazing Top Three Book (T3) community. Anyone thinking of writing a book needs a copy of her book, *Write a Must Read*, and should check out all her online offerings.

I'd also like to thank all the people who read this workbook early and gave feedback: Beth May—copy editor extraordinaire!, Pat Gouhin, Jules Apollo, Vickie Lanthier, Lisa Dyson, Cynthia Beiler, Amy Jacobs, Glory Enyinnaya, Miki Feldman Simon, Amanda Gibson, Susan Barber, Lisa Nirell, Carolyn Jungclas, Dana Wichterman and, of course, Sue Bevan Baggott, who helped immensely.

AUTHOR BIO

Marcia Dawood is an early-stage investor who serves on the Securities and Exchange Commission's Small Business Capital Formation Advisory Committee, and is a venture partner with Mindshift Capital, a member of Golden Seeds, and the chair emeritus of the Angel Capital Association (ACA), a global professional society for angel investors.

A TEDx speaker and the host of *The Angel Next Door* podcast, Marcia walks the talk and holds investments in over fifty early-stage companies and funds. She is committed to expanding support for diverse companies that overcome the world's biggest problems and accelerate positive change.

She is also an associate producer on the award-winning documentary film *Show Her the Money*, which debuted at the Women's Film Festival in Philadelphia in September 2023.

She is a founding member and chair of the ACA's Growing Women's Capital Group, which is building syndication and collaboration among US investment groups focused on women-led companies.

Previously, Marcia worked in sales, marketing, and operations for Kaplan Education for over sixteen years. She received an MBA from the University of North Carolina Kenan-Flagler Business School.

Marcia currently lives in North Carolina with her husband, Izzy, and she feels lucky to be the stepmom to three amazing sons.

www.ingramcontent.com/pod-product-compliance
Lightning Source LLC
Chambersburg PA
CBHW082246090526
44585CB00021BA/2462